Introducing Dart Sass

A Practical Introduction to
the Replacement for Sass,
Built on Dart

Alex Libby

Apress®

Introducing Dart Sass

Alex Libby
Rugby, Warwickshire, UK

ISBN-13 (pbk): 978-1-4842-4371-8   ISBN-13 (electronic): 978-1-4842-4372-5
https://doi.org/10.1007/978-1-4842-4372-5

Library of Congress Control Number: 2019932808

Managing Director, Apress Media LLC: Welmoed Spahr
Acquisitions Editor: Louise Corrigan
Development Editor: James Markham
Coordinating Editor: Nancy Chen

Cover designed by eStudioCalamar

Cover image designed by Freepik (www.freepik.com)

Distributed to the book trade worldwide by Springer Science+Business Media New York, 233 Spring Street, 6th Floor, New York, NY 10013. Phone 1-800-SPRINGER, fax (201) 348-4505, e-mail orders-ny@springer-sbm.com, or visit www.springeronline.com. Apress Media, LLC is a California LLC and the sole member (owner) is Springer Science + Business Media Finance Inc (SSBM Finance Inc). SSBM Finance Inc is a **Delaware** corporation.

For information on translations, please e-mail rights@apress.com, or visit http://www.apress.com/rights-permissions.

Apress titles may be purchased in bulk for academic, corporate, or promotional use. eBook versions and licenses are also available for most titles. For more information, reference our Print and eBook Bulk Sales web page at http://www.apress.com/bulk-sales.

Any source code or other supplementary material referenced by the author in this book is available to readers on GitHub via the book's product page, located at www.apress.com/9781484243718. For more detailed information, please visit http://www.apress.com/source-code.

Printed on acid-free paper

This is dedicated to my family, with thanks for their love and support whilst writing this book.

Table of Contents

About the Author

Alex Libby is an A/B testing developer and seasoned computer book author who hails from England. His passion for all things Open Source dates back to the days of his degree studies, where he first came across web development, and has been hooked ever since. His daily work involves extensive use of JavaScript, HTML, and CSS to manipulate existing website content; Alex enjoys tinkering with different open source libraries to see how they work. He has spent a stint maintaining the jQuery Tools library and enjoys writing about Open Source technologies, principally for front-end UI development. Away from developing code, Alex enjoys managing stage shows, photography, or being out and about cycling around his hometown on his bike.

About the Technical Reviewer

 **Ferit Topcu** is a software developer who has been enjoying the last years working and exploring the Web and JavaScript. He's been in web development for five+ years and has worked in different areas from researching topics, social media analytics, and Internet of Things, to recently joining one of Europe's biggest e-commerce companies – Zalando. There he is developing web applications to improve the whole retail process.

Acknowledgments

Writing a book can be a long but rewarding process; it is not possible to complete it without the help of other people. I would like to offer a huge vote of thanks to my editors – in particular, Nancy Chen and Louise Corrigan; my thanks also to Ferit Topcu as my technical reviewer, and James Markham for his help during the process. All four have made writing this book a painless and enjoyable process, even with the edits.

My thanks also to my family for being understanding and supporting me while writing – I frequently spend lots of late nights writing alone, so their words of encouragement have been a real help in getting past those bumps in the road and producing the finished book that you now hold in your hands.

Introduction

Introducing Dart Sass is for people who want to quickly create valid CSS styles for use within websites.

Originally written in Ruby, and released back in 2006, this new version has been rewritten from ground up to be faster and simpler to use, yet still retain the same features that users of Sass have come to know and love.

Over the course of this book, I'll take you on a journey through using the library, showing you how easy it is to quickly create reusable styles with the minimum of fuss – we'll cover such diverse topics as operations, string interpolation, creating and manipulating content using functions, and more, with lots of simple exercises to help develop your skills using Sass as a tool.

Introducing Dart Sass is for the website developer who is keen to learn how to quickly leverage the power of Sass to produce valid style sheet code, where pressure is on to produce results rapidly. It's perfect for those in Agile teams where time is of the essence, or for developers keen to build reusable styles to help save development time and resources for present and future projects.

CHAPTER 1

Introducing Sass

Imagine the scene if you will – it's late on Friday, and you're ready to go home. Only your boss walks up to your desk and says there's a last-minute change needed on some styles for the buttons in your latest project. Ugh – so much for finishing on time. …

Sound familiar? Ordinarily, we might have to spend hours poring through style sheets, working out which styles to change and where, hoping that we don't miss anything in our hunt. This is a real drag, particularly when you had hopes to go on a night out – no problem if you use Sass!

The term "Sass" has been floating around for a few years, with some well-known names as proponents of the technology. The real question I'll bet you're asking though is this: What is all of the hype about, and how will it help in my development?

What Is Sass?

These are two very good questions ask to really understand what Sass is all about; however, we must first answer one question: What is a CSS preprocessor?

Put simply, a preprocessor is a scripting language that we can use to extend CSS; we use it to write code in one language before compiling it into CSS. Sass is arguably the most popular of these although others exist, such as Less or Stylus. Sass allows us to create all types of shortcuts: from simple placeholders to update multiple instances of a single value, through to creating new styles that subsume existing base styles.

© Alex Libby 2019
A. Libby, *Introducing Dart Sass*, https://doi.org/10.1007/978-1-4842-4372-5_1

So now that we've been introduced to preprocessors, it's time we answered those two questions: What is Sass all about, and how is it going to help in my development?

First appearing back in 2006 and created by Hampton Catlin, Sass, or Syntactically Awesome Stylesheets (yes, it is a bit of a mouthful), is billed as an extension of CSS. It brings in the power of basic scripting tools such as variables and loops, to help keep your code more organized and create style sheets faster than with ordinary CSS. If the thought of creating variables or loops scares you, then don't worry – they are much easier to use than the terms might imply! We will go through all of the core functions of Sass over the course of this book; by the end, you will be more at ease with Sass and wonder why you hadn't made the change to using it sooner.

Okay – let's move on: now that we've been formally introduced, let's answer the second question: How is Sass going to help me when it comes to developing style sheets?

Understanding the Advantages of Using Sass

When working with Sass over time, it would be easy to understand why some consider it to be a real Swiss army knife of a toolbox. Although it contains a healthy selection of tools, its power is only really limited by one's imagination! Taking a step back, though, there are some key advantages to using the library, so let's take a look at them in detail:

- Sass allows us to break large style sheet files into smaller, more manageable files; we can work on individual files and let Sass compile all of them into one larger file. Take a look at WordPress, for example – it's lengthy style sheet (which weighs in at 4,500+ lines) makes use of Sass to help break this monster into smaller, easier-to-edit files.

- Traditional development might have involved us creating multiple style sheets, particularly if we're catering for specific browsers, such as IE9 or below. Although this principle works, it results in increased HTTP requests, which all require resources. Sass allows us to make use of the @import statement to not only break the style sheet into smaller files, but which also helps to reduce the number of HTTP requests made to the server.

- One of the most important benefits of Sass, though, is reducing repetition. Put simply, we can create styles that are extensions of existing ones; the new ones contain the same attributes as the base style, without us having to repeat them.

- We can incorporate as little or as much of Sass-style code into our style sheet as we like; Sass will ignore any standard CSS rules, so as long as the file structure is in place, then we can update rules in stages, and not in one large change.

- Another benefit of using Sass is the ability to create variables or placeholders for values. These placeholders can be reused throughout our projects – if we need to change a value, we change it once, and this ripples throughout the style sheet during compilation. A great example of this comes when working with colors – if we need to change a shade of red, for example, we can do it once; Sass updates each instance of this shade throughout our style sheet automatically.

Okay – enough chitchat: it's time to get stuck into the detail! We've explored a number of key benefits of using Sass; these will come to life throughout the course of this book. But – as they say – we must start somewhere, and the best place is with the different syntaxes and implementations available when using Sass, and why it really pays to take care when writing Sass code…

The Different Syntaxes of Sass

Hold on – did you just say different … *syntaxes*? Yes, you heard correctly: Sass does indeed have two syntaxes, but before you run to the hills, don't fret. We're not going to learn both! It's worth clarifying what is available though, so let me explain:

- The original, or indented syntax, uses something similar to the Haml scripting language – it uses indentation to separate code blocks and newline characters to separate rules. This uses the `.sass` file extension.

- The newer syntax, "SCSS" (or Sassy CSS), uses block formatting similar to that of CSS; it uses braces to denote code blocks and semicolons to separate lines within a block. This uses the `.scss` file extension.

To complicate matters further, there are also different implementations of Sass available, including ones written in C, PHP, and Java – it's no wonder things might seem a little confusing!

Throughout the course of this book, we'll use the latest version of Sass, which has been rewritten using Dart; you may see references to Ruby Sass, but this has been deprecated in favor of Dart Sass, and it will go out of support. At the same time, we will use the newer syntax – its proximity to vanilla CSS makes it much easier to learn.

The original syntax for Sass is still available – it requires the use of indents and newline characters to format code, which makes it harder to learn for those new to using Sass.

Okay – hopefully that has cleared up some of the confusion about the various implementations of Sass; it's time we moved on and got stuck into more practical matters! There is no better place to start than to get ourselves set up with Sass; before we do so, there is a little housekeeping task we must perform first.

Some Project Housekeeping

When you start on a project for the first time, there is nearly always some form of housekeeping to be done, right?

Well, we're not going to break with tradition here – we have one simple task to do: go ahead and create a folder called dart-sass, which we will use to store the code from each exercise throughout this book. It doesn't matter where it is stored, although I will assume for our purposes that it is stored at the root of your PC or laptop; we'll refer to it as our project folder throughout this book. With that in place, let's make a start on our first exercise, which is to install and configure Sass for use.

Setting Up Sass

Although we talk of "setting up" Sass, there is nothing complicated to do – there are very few steps involved! Gone are the days of having to install big dependencies such as Ruby (if you happened to have used older versions of Sass); the Dart version of Sass is based entirely on JavaScript so is a cinch to install.

5

Over the course of the next few pages, we'll go through the process step by step – at the end of this chapter you will have a basic system in place that can easily be extended, along with an understanding of what is required to work with Sass.

INSTALLING SASS

Let's make a start on installing Sass:

1. We'll start by downloading Sass from `https://github.com/sass/dart-sass/releases/`; make sure you choose the appropriate version for your platform. Save the compressed file into a new folder called `firstcompile`, at the root of our project area.

2. Next, open the compressed file, and extract the contents into the same `firstcompile` folder.

3. We now need to add the location to your `Path` variable for your platform.

If you're unsure how to do this, then take a look at the appendix at the end of this book, which details the procedure for Mac, Windows, and Linux platforms.

---

4. We're ready to test that Sass has been installed correctly – for this, fire up a terminal session and change the working folder to the `firstcompile` folder we created in step 1.

5. At the prompt, enter `sass --version` and press Enter – if all
    is well, we should see it return a number, indicating the version
    installed, similar to that shown in Figure 1-1.

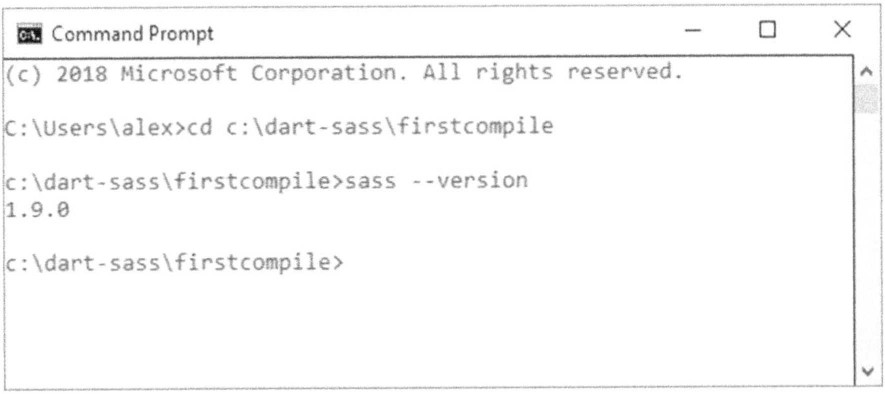

```
Command Prompt                                    —    □    ✕
(c) 2018 Microsoft Corporation. All rights reserved.

C:\Users\alex>cd c:\dart-sass\firstcompile

c:\dart-sass\firstcompile>sass --version
1.9.0

c:\dart-sass\firstcompile>
```

Figure 1-1. *Checking that Sass is installed*

6. For now, keep the terminal node session open – we will revert
    back to it very shortly in the next exercise.

That was really easy – if you were expecting more, then I am sorry to
disappoint! There's no need to install any dependencies (unlike in the days
of working with Ruby Sass, which required Ruby); instead, it's just a matter
of unzipping an archive file in a folder of our choice.

This is all very well, but as they say, the proof of the pudding is in its
tasting – it's only good if it compiles a Sass file to valid CSS! This should
be a formality though: to prove this is indeed the case, let's take a look at
testing the compilation process in more detail.

OUR FIRST COMPILATION

At this stage don't worry if the Sass code doesn't make sense just yet – all we're interested in is making sure that our compilation process produces a valid style sheet. We have a couple of steps to go through, so let's make a start:

1. First, go ahead and open a new document in your usual text editor, and add the following lines. Don't worry about them not making sense just yet; we will go into detail at the end of the exercise:

   ```
   $font-stack: Helvetica, sans-serif;
   $primary-color: #ccc;
   $decoration-color: #0cf;

   body { font: 100% $font-stack; color: $primary-color;
   text-decoration-color: $decoration-color}
   ```

2. Save this as test.scss at the root of our dart-sass folder, then go ahead and fire up a terminal session.

3. Change the working folder to your dart-sass folder, then enter this command and press Enter:

   ```
   sass test.scss output.css
   ```

4. At this stage, we won't see any message appear to confirm success – for this, we need to look in our dart-sass folder, where we can see two new files have appeared, plus our test.scss file (Figure 1-2).

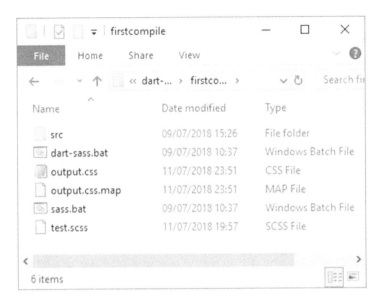

Figure 1-2. *Our first compilation*

See how easy that was? Granted, our demo did make use of a terminal session, which might scare some; there are ways to get around this, which we will go through later in this chapter. For now, our demo has touched on some key points we should explore, so let's break down our compilation process in more detail, to understand how we arrived at our compiled style sheet.

Understanding What Happened

At first glance, our demo looks simple enough (at least in terms of quantity), even if we might not be sure about exactly what has taken place! Let me reveal all – our demo has covered two key steps upon which we will elaborate later in this book. For now, they can be summarized as the following:

- Compiling code from Sass to CSS,

- Creating and reusing variables (or placeholders).

Let's first take a look at the compilation process – at a very basic level, we simply need to specify a source file (in this case, test.scss), and the name of the output file we want to create (output.css). It doesn't matter where we run the compilation process – the key things, though, are that we clearly specify the right file names, and that the Sass compiler will automatically replace existing files in the destination folder.

We touched on the second key point being the creation of variables – this might seem a little scary for those of you not familiar with programming techniques, but trust me: they are easier to use than it might sound! If we take a look at the contents of test.scss, we will see the code listed in Figure 1-3.

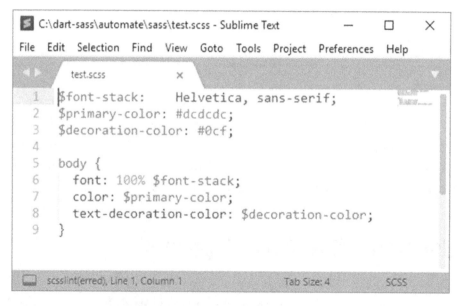

Figure 1-3. *Examining our source Sass file ...*

> Sass will not attempt to try to compile CSS rules already in the Sass file; these will be copied across to the destination file untouched. It's a useful point to bear in mind – we will explore why, later in this book.

Let's go though it line by line –

- We then open a rule for body – inside of which we specify properties for font, font color, and text decoration. Instead of specifying fixed values, we've inserted placeholders that correspond to the variables listed in lines 1 to 3 of our code.

- Our first three lines specify placeholder values, or **variables** – one for our font-family name, with two for colors (one as the font color, and the second as a text-decoration color). Sass is pretty flexible when it comes to naming conventions; you can use any name that is appropriate, as long as it is not an existing keyword; any variable must start with a $ symbol to signify it as such.

Think of variables as buckets or placeholders – these tell Sass where to insert the real value during compilation. To prove this, go ahead and open up output.css; inside you will see our three properties now have human-readable values, as indicated in Figure 1-4.

Figure 1-4. *... and the output file*

The compilation process performs a number of tasks, one of which is replacing variables with proper values. Our example only had three, but imagine if this were repeated multiple times in a lengthy style sheet (such as WordPress)? At a stroke, we can update a single instance of a variable and recompile our file – we eliminate any risk of missing a variable, as Sass will update every instance it finds automatically.

We will revisit the concept of variables in Chapter 2, "Introducing Variables and Mixins."

Okay – let's change tack: our process works, but it will get a little tedious if we have to continue compiling code by hand all of the time. In addition, we can definitely improve on our folder structure; it's time we took a look at how we might set up a suitable workflow to help with the compilation process.

Setting Up a Workflow

When working with Sass, it pays to be organized – we might get away with what we've set up thus far if we're only going to work on a couple of files. If, however, we need to work on anything more substantial, then this clearly won't work: it's time we got ourselves organized.

I'm a great believer in keeping things simple – after all, there is no benefit in making something more complicated than it needs to be! There are a few changes we can make that will certainly help us, so let's take a look:

- Setting up a suitable folder structure to store our assets,

- Enabling CSS source map support,

- Automating the compilation process,

- Adjusting the output format of our code,

- Making sure we have a good text editor available.

We will add to this over the course of this book, by exploring ways of producing reusable code, or extra tips to help with the development process. The important thing to understand though is that although we may not need anything complicated to get started, it is important to get them configured correctly; let's dive in and explore this in more detail.

Setting Up a Folder Structure

I would absolutely recommend creating a folder structure to store your assets; as a starting point, I would suggest one folder for Sass source files and another for the compiled CSS style sheet files. One of the key benefits of Sass is the ability to break a larger style sheet into smaller files; over time we could build up a folder structure similar to that shown in Figure 1-5.

```
1    sass/
2    |- _base/
3    |    |- _config.scss
4    |    |- _presets.scss
5    |    |- _headings.scss
6    |    |- ...
7
8    |- _layouts/
9    |    |- _l-base.scss
10   |    |- _l-grid.scss
11
12   |- _modules/
13   |    |- _m-buttons.scss
14   |    |- _m-tabs.scss
15
16   |- application.scss
17
18   stylesheets/
19   |- application.css
20
21
```

Figure 1-5. *A typical folder structure for Sass development*

Of course, this takes time to develop, so if we start with a simple folder for source files (in this example, sass), and a separate one (such as stylesheets from our example), then this will put us in good stead for developing Sass code.

Enabling Source Map Support

Take another look at the bottom of our compiled test.css file – did you notice the presence of this line?

```
/*# sourceMappingURL=maps/test.css.map */
```

This is a link to a CSS source map – this is an indispensable tool when it comes to working with Sass. Put simply, it translates each compiled rule in our style sheet back to the original Sass code; we can use it to identify exactly where an issue might be in our code.

Source maps are automatically produced when compiling via the command line (or terminal session). To use them, we have to enable browser support – let's run through how, using Chrome as our example browser:

- Fire up the browser and then press Ctrl + Shift + I (or Command + Apple + I for Macs), to bring up the Developer Console.

- Click on the three dots to the top right of Console, then hit Settings.

- Look for the Enable CSS source maps entry, under Sources (Figure 1-6).

Figure 1-6. *Enabling CSS source maps option*

If you take a look at Figure 1-2 again, you'll see the presence of a output.css.map file – this was created automatically when we compiled our first file on the command line. Opening the file in a text editor, we will see something akin to this:

```
{"version":3,"sourceRoot":"","sources":["../sass/test.scss"],
"names":[],"mappings":"AAIA;EACE;EACA,OALc;EAMd,uBALiB","file":
"output.css"}
```

It probably looks like meaningless code, but it contains mappings from the compiled CSS file (`output.css`), which point to the relevant code within our original source file, `test.scss`. Suffice to say that we don't need to worry about what is produced inside this file – the compilation process takes care of this for us. As long as one is present, and support is enabled in our browser, we will be able to relate compiled code back to its original source.

Automating the Compilation Process

In the *Our first compilation* demo, we used this line to compile our code:

```
sass test.scss output.css
```

It's a simple command – it does the job with no frills, assuming of course we've written valid Sass code! However, running this each time will quickly get tedious; we can absolutely improve on this, by use of the `--watch` parameter.

This requires a simple change to our command – it's almost worth getting into the habit of including it when running a compile from a terminal session! Instead of the command we used, we can use this:

```
sass --watch test.scss output.css
```

This will watch for changes and recompile our source file automatically – there is something we need to look out for though, but I will cover this in Chapter 2.

Adjusting the Output Format

If you take a look at a compiled CSS file, you may notice that Sass has produced something that is easy to read but takes a lot of space. This clearly isn't ideal for use in production sites – we want our files to be as small as possible! Fortunately there's an easy change we can make to our compilation process – remember our first compile command, which looked like this?

```
sass test.scss output.css
```

If we add in the command highlighted in bold:

```
sass test.scss output.css --style=compressed
```

... this will compress our compiled style sheet, which will be ideal for use on production sites.

By default, if you omit this command, Sass will produce code in expanded format – if you prefer to specify this explicitly, then use `--style=expanded` instead.

Editing Sass Code

Now – this might seem like an odd point to pick up on, but you'll understand why in a moment: although there is a good selection of tools that we can use to edit Sass code, we don't necessarily need them! Let me explain what I mean:

At a basic level, Sass is nothing more than an extension of CSS – it means that pretty much any text editor can be used to edit Sass code. I suspect many of you will already have a favorite editor that will work fine with Sass. I personally use Sublime Text 3, which is a commercial offering, but the 80USD price tag is definitely worth the price!

For the purposes of this book, I will assume you already have a suitable editor that already works well for you. If not, then it helps to have one that has syntax support for Sass and can open and format multiple files (not really a problem, as most do anyway). If you don't already have something, then one of these might be a good place to start:

- Atom (cross platform) – available from https://atom.io/

- TextMate (Mac OS only) – https://macromates.com

- Sublime Text (cross platform, commercial) – downloadable from https://www.sublimetext.com

- Visual Code (cross platform, free) – available from https://code.visualstudio.com/

However, there is another option that will really turn things on their head: if you want to use a dedicated **stand-alone** tool for compiling Sass, then there is also a mix of open source and commercial offerings available. Some will work across multiple platforms, while others target specific platforms only. Let's take a look at some of the options open to us:

- CodeKit – this commercial offering is available from https://codekitapp.com/ but is for Mac only

- GhostLab – available as a commercial application for Mac or Windows, from http://www.vanamco.com/ghostlab/

- Hammer – a Mac-only commercial editor, available from https://hammerformac.com/

- Koala – downloadable from http://koala-app.com/, Koala is a cross-platform, open source editor, although it has not seen any updates since late 2017

- Prepos – this shareware editor is available from https://prepros.io/ with versions available for Mac, Windows, and Linux

- Scout-App – an open source editor available for Mac, Windows, and Linux, downloadable from http://scout-app.io/

Note   "All" in the above list refers to Mac, Windows, and Linux support.

Oh – and guess what? There's yet another route to compiling Sass that we can choose! If your preference is to not install yet another tool into your development workflow, then you can always choose to compile your code online.

There are several options available for this, but one that is recommended is SassMeister, hosted at `https://www.sassmeister.com`. This gives you all of the benefit of compiling Sass in exactly the same way as if we were doing so offline; it's probably less suited to compiling lengthy, complex blocks of code, but ideal if you want to try ideas out before committing changes to your source code.

Making a Choice

I'm sure the question on everyone's mind is this: With all of those options, how do I choose which one to use?

The short but simple answer is this: it depends. I know this might sound like a cop-out, but there is no right or wrong answer to how Sass should be compiled. It all depends on what you already have installed, what you feel comfortable using, and (to a lesser extent) which platform you use.

For example, if you prefer using a visual approach, then using one of the editors with dedicated support (such as Prepos), then this will work fine. However, if you happen to use Node.js, then it makes sense to consider adapting your workflow to incorporate a step for compiling Sass. You might equally not want to have to install anything extra at all – in this case, using a terminal approach is the simplest route (and doesn't require installing!). The key point being though is that there are plenty of ways of editing Sass – don't be afraid to try out different applications until you find one that you like and works well for you.

For the purposes of this book, I will use the terminal approach to keep things simple and the focus on Sass code, not the compiling process – please feel free to switch to using a visual editor if you prefer to use this option.

Okay – let's move on; there is another part of this process we should consider. Remember how I said it can be a pain to have to recompile code manually all of the time? Well, we can automate the process using a task runner such as Gulp – let's take a look at what is involved in more detail.

Automating the Process

Although compiling Sass code manually is fine for light development, it will soon become a pain for anything much larger! Surely there has to be a better way to do this ... absolutely – we could use a dedicated application such as Koala or Prepos, or even compile directly in the browser, using SassMeister. However, it will become tedious when switching between applications; it also opens the risk of making mistakes in our code!

There is an alternative: Why not *automate* the compilation process? Sure, it's not essential for developing Sass code, but creating something that can deal with low-value tasks, such as compiling, presents several benefits:

- We can set it up to run in the background – any changes we make to code will be compiled automatically for us;

- We can link in other tasks as part of the process, such as compressing JavaScript files or adding vendor prefixes to style rules;

- It removes the need for us to be involved in tasks of low value, allowing us to spend more time on important matters.

With this in mind, our next exercise will set up an automatic compilation process using Gulp and the gulp-dart-sass package, the latter of which is a wrapper for the Dart Sass library. Once installed and running, this will then happily sit running in the background; as soon as changes to a Sass file are noted, it will automatically compile them into a valid CSS style sheet file. Let's take a look at what is involved in more detail.

AUTOMATING PROCESS

Task runners such as Gulp need to be installed using the Node.js runtime environment – this is available for the Windows, Mac, and Linux platforms, with binaries available for others. We have a few steps to run through, so let's make a start:

1. The first step is to install Node.js – for this, head over to `https://nodejs.org`, and download the version appropriate for your platform. If prompted, accept all defaults; this is sufficient for the purposes of this exercise.

2. Once installed, fire up a terminal session and enter this command to confirm Node and NPM have been successfully installed:

   ```
   node -v && npm -v
   ```

   If all is well, Node will return `v8.11.3` or higher, and NPM (Node's package manager) will display `5.6.0` or higher.

3. Next, run this command at the prompt – it turns off the creation of `package-lock.json` files, which are a new feature of NPM version 5 or above, but are not needed for the demos in this book:

   ```
   npm config set package-lock false
   ```

4. Now go ahead and extract a copy of the automate folder to your project area.

5. We have a few things to install, so for this, fire up terminal session, and first run this command – this will install dependencies for Gulp:

```
npm install -g gulp-cli
```

6. Once completed, go ahead and run this command at the prompt – this will install the remaining packages (Sass, Gulp, Sourcemap support and Autoprefixer for Gulp – a PostCSS tool, but works fine with standard CSS) listed in the package. json file we copied over in the automate folder, as shown in Figure 1-7.

```
npm install
```

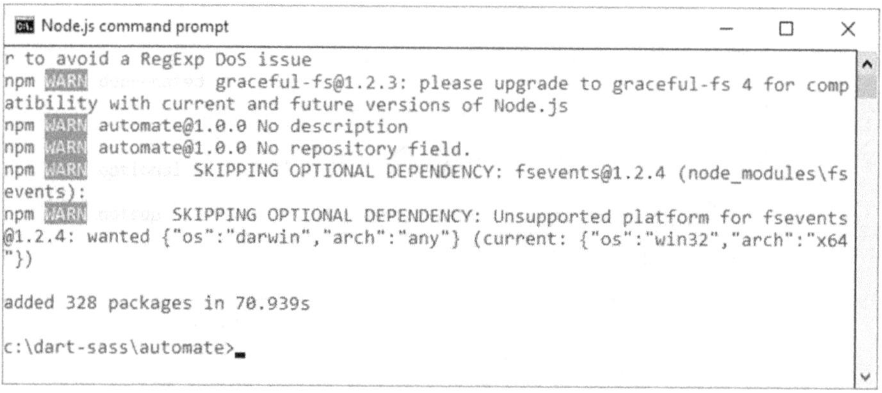

Figure 1-7. *Installing our packages*

The warnings about fsevents and deprecated packages can be ignored for the purposes of this exercise.

At this stage, our automated process is set up; let's put it to the test by editing our test file, and watch it compile. For this next step, I would recommend having the sass and css folders open on screen, along with our terminal session:

7. Go ahead and enter gulp at the prompt, then press Enter.

8. The initial default task is run – this can be ignored. Open test. scss in the sass folder, and change the hex code assigned to $primary-color to #dcdcdc (a light gray color) .

9. Save the change – if all is well, Gulp's watch facility will kick in and automatically recompile our code, as shown in Figure 1-8.

```
gulp                                               —     □     ×

c:\dart-sass\automate>gulp
[20:30:54] Using gulpfile
[20:30:54] Starting 'default'...
[20:30:54] Finished 'default' after

[watcher] File sass\test.scss was changed, compiling...
[20:32:58] Starting 'sass'...
[20:32:58] Finished 'sass' after
```

Figure 1-8. *Recompiling our code automatically*

10. Take a look inside the css folder – you will now see a newly compiled style sheet and map folder, which contains our source map file.

Hopefully that wasn't too painful – it may seem like a good few steps, but it opens up a host of possibilities for later development. That aside, our process covers a number of key points that we should be aware of, so let's dive in and break down what happened in more detail.

Breaking Down Our Process

Over the course of the last few pages, we've created a basic system that can automatically compile Sass, using the power of Node.js (and its package manager, NPM). To achieve this, we've installed Node and some NPM packages using some preconfigured instruction files. Let's take a look at these instruction files in detail, starting with **package.json**.

The package.json file contains details of all of the packages we will use – in this case, we've specified Gulp as our task runner, along with gulp-sourcemaps (to provide source maps), our obligatory gulp-dart-sass (for Sass support), and gulp-autoprefixer (to add or remove vendor prefixes as needed). You will notice that the exercise didn't run through the install for each separately: this is by design. It's more efficient to run npm install that will look for the presence of any package.json file in the same folder and install listed packages within, by default. It does require some pre-work to create our package.json file beforehand, but this will simplify the installation process.

Exploring the specifics of setting up the package.json is outside of the scope of this book – if you are interested in learning more, then I would recommend heading over to https://docs.npmjs.com/getting-started/using-a-package.json for more details.

Once the packages were installed, we then made use of the **gulpfile.js** file to perform the compilation. This file contains a set of instructions to perform each time it detects the presence of a file change within our targeted folder. Let's take a look at that code, starting with a handful of declarations – the first is to enforce strict error checking:

```
'use strict';
```

We then set up some require declarations to various packages, which are called as and when required:

```
var gulp = require('gulp');
var sass = require('gulp-dart-sass');
var sourcemaps = require('gulp-sourcemaps');
var autoprefixer = require('gulp-autoprefixer');
```

The next block down is our sass task – this takes care of compiling our source files into valid CSS style sheet files:

```
gulp.task('sass', function () {
  return gulp.src('sass/*.scss')
    .pipe(autoprefixer({ browsers: ['last 2 versions'] }))
    .pipe(sourcemaps.init('/maps'))
    .pipe(sass().on('error', sass.logError))
    .pipe(sourcemaps.write('./maps'))
    .pipe(gulp.dest('./css')) ;
});
```

It starts off by targeting files in the sass folder with the scss extension; this is to prevent the compiler from trying to work on files that are not valid Sass source files! The next step is to then add vendor prefixes for CSS properties that are yet to be standardized; in this case, we're supporting the latest two releases of each browser.

The next step is the crucial one – this takes care of the compilation process; it will either compile our file or display any errors it encounters on screen. We then finish off by creating the appropriate source map file (in a similar way to when we compiled in a terminal session), before writing the files to disk (in the css subfolder).

As an aside – by default, the output format will be expanded; if we want to change the output format, then alter the code as indicated: sass({outputStyle: 'compressed'}).

None of this will work without the final task – the default one runs as soon as we enter gulp at the terminal session prompt. This watches out for any Sass files within the sass folder; any changes made will trigger the sass task:

```
gulp.task('default', function () {
  gulp.watch('sass/*.scss', ['sass'])
  .on('change', function(evt) {
    console.log(
      '\n[watcher] File ' + evt.path.replace(/.*(?=sass)/,") +
      ' was ' + evt.type + ', compiling...'
    );
  });
});
```

As soon as a change is made, we call a small function to display a message to confirm a named file has been changed; the code is then recompiled before saved to disk as new style sheet and map files.

Ultimately this might seem a lot of work to get set up, but it is important to note that you may have part of this in place already. It's just one way of automating our compilation process; you might prefer to use something like Grunt or Webpack instead. The aim, though, is to consider what you may or may not already have, whether you have any preferences (if you've used a task runner before), and to decide if the nature of your projects mean that you can benefit from automating the process.

As an aside, it's worth noting that I will use this process for exercises throughout this book, unless specified otherwise. This is just personal preference; please feel free to use whichever compilation process works best for you.

Right – enough chitchat: time to change tack! Hopefully you'll have tried a few options and have found something that works for you, or is at least working. It's time we focused more on Sass itself, so without further ado, let's begin with covering some of the key terms you will meet when working with Sass.

Getting Acquainted with Key Terms

Over the course of this book, we'll meet a host of different techniques and key terms when working with Sass – some will be easy to get to grips with, while others may take a little more time!

We've already met the most important one – the compilation process. For us, it's less about understanding the internal machinations of *how* it works, as it is a bit of a black box of tricks, so to speak! It's more important to gain *an appreciation* of what we can do – for example, if we're creating a set of buttons, we can write code that automates much of this for us, which Sass will compile (or transform) into valid CSS code.

Compiling isn't the only concept we cover, though – Sass has a number of key terms that we will explore throughout this book. Although many of these terms won't mean anything just yet, I thought I would summarize some of the key ones here, so you can get a feel for what to expect later in the book. I will also include the relevant chapter number, so if you get stuck, you know which chapter to turn to for help:

- Comments – this is one of the simplest techniques to use in Sass; it works just in the same way as you would for normal CSS. The key to using them though is in the type of comment you use – for example, single line comments are removed during compilation, while multi-line comments are preserved. We'll cover this in more detail in the section "Adding Comments," in Chapter 2.

- Variables – think of these as placeholders for values; Sass looks for every single instance of a particular variable and replaces it with the real value that we set up at the start. It doesn't matter how many instances we have of a particular variable in our code – Sass replaces them all! We'll talk more on this subject in the section "Creating Variables in a Practical Context," in Chapter 2.

- Mixins – variables are a good start, but what if we wanted to define bigger blocks of code in the same way? Step up mixins – these act as predefined blocks of code we can literally "mix in" to our code. We can define them once and reuse them in multiple projects – turn to Chapter 2 to learn more about this useful technique.

- Importing and Partials – if you've ever had to work on large spreadsheets (such as the monster that is WordPress, at 4,500+ lines!), then you will know only too well how painful it can get when managing so many lines of code. Sass has an @import function, similar to CSS; we can use it to create partials or fragments of CSS code that we can import to our main style sheet. We'll cover this, and more, in Chapter 2.

- Nesting – how many times have you written CSS code for something such as a menu system, only to find yourself repeating multiple styles? Well, with Sass, we can nest styles within a style – think of it as grouping styles together, inside a base style that is common to all. In a sense it's a form of shorthand, which makes it easier to read the code – we'll cover this in Chapter 3, "Creating Nesting Styles."

- Inheritance – this is a little more tricker: instead of rewriting code blocks with similar properties multiple times, how about inheriting one from another? A perfect example is creating buttons – we can write a base style rule to cover attributes such as size and font. Any buttons we create can then inherit this base style, plus any we specify for each button, such as its color. It's a great technique to learn but takes time to really master – we'll start that journey in Chapter 3, "Creating Nesting Styles."

- Operators – I suspect in many cases you might specify fixed values in your spreadsheet, such as 16px for a font-size attribute, right? What if we could work out values *dynamically*, using nothing more than simple operations such as addition or subtraction? Gone are the days when we might have to specify a whole set of color palette values, for example – as long as we have one, we can use a little math to work out complementary colors automatically. I'll reveal how, and more, in Chapter 4, "Calculating Values Using Operations."

- Directives – this is where things get really interesting! CSS already has several @-rules; Sass adds to these with some such as @extend or @media. Think of these as rules that help control the flow and logic in your Sass code – a great example is @media, which we use to specify which rules to apply for responsive site development. We'll dive in to the world of directives in Chapter 4, "Calculating Values Using Operations."

Phew – there's a real bunch of exciting techniques coming our way! Of course, we don't have to cover them in all in one go – the great thing about Sass is that we can start with simple techniques such as setting up variables, then gradually make use of more tools as we develop our style sheets. Before we start on that journey, though, there is one topic that I know will be of most benefit to anyone starting with Sass – where I can I get help if something isn't working or I get stuck?

Getting Help

"Help! Why is my mixin not performing as it should …?"

Although Sass is relatively easy to learn, there will come a time when you need help – sure, there are lots of people online who have written about Sass, but sometimes it helps to have someone get you out of that sticky problem! Don't worry – there are several ways of getting help; they include the following:

- If you're stuck on something, and am struggling to get it working, then your first port of call should be the StackOverflow site, at `https://stackoverflow.com`. This is managed by a community of volunteers, where anyone can post a question; I would strongly recommend reading the guidelines available at `https://stackoverflow.com/help/` to help improve the likelihood of getting a response that helps solve your issue.

It's also worth running a quick search to see if anyone else has come across the same issue – try `https://stackoverflow.com/search?q=Dart+Sass;` you never know, someone may already know the answer! Please be patient though: it is a volunteer operation, so you may not get a response quickly.

- If, however, you think you've identified a bug, where behavior is not working as advertised or a core function is clearly faulty, then GitHub is a good place to report them. The GitHub site for Dart Sass is at `https://github.com/sass/dart-sass` – make sure you get the right one though, as the Sass team run several GitHub site for different versions of Sass.

If you do need to raise an issue, it can seem a little daunting if you've not done it before. It's worth noting that GitHub sites are often maintained by volunteers who have seen issues before, and they are always willing to help. There are some useful tips you can follow to help with the process of logging an issue:

- Do have a good look through past issues – it is possible (although not always) that someone has already logged a similar problem, which may help you, without the need to raise one yourself.

- Do add a title and description, and be as detailed
  as you can about the issue – include screenshots,
  steps to reproduce, what you've tried so far, and the
  results, but don't write an encyclopedia! GitHub
  volunteers' time is precious, so keeping it detailed
  but concise is essential.

- Please be polite and courteous when posting – GitHub
  sites are run by volunteers who have families and
  paid jobs, and who are less likely to help you if you
  are rude. If you treat them with respect, then they will
  only be too happy to help guide you.

- If you've discovered something that you consider
  to be a bug, but the response is that it is "by design,"
  then please respect their decision. If however you
  feel strongly, then politely present your case, with
  detail, and be willing to discuss the merits of your
  points. Maintainers can't cater for all circumstances
  and will always consider new evidence, but they
  won't be willing to help if you are abusive or rude.
  Equally, if a maintainer has reviewed your request
  but come to the decision that no changes should be
  made, then please respect their decision.

- Please allow a reasonable amount of time before
  chasing a response – people may have other
  commitments, or time differences may get in the
  way; you need to allow for this when posting issues.

- Always try to respond quickly if suggestions have
  been made to help you; no one likes responding to
  an issue only to find you can't be bothered to try
  things out!

I could go on, but most of these guidelines can really be summarized into three key points: always be polite and respectful, make sure you have sufficient detail around your issue, and respond in a timely manner when appropriate. As long as you follow these guidelines, then plenty of people will be willing to help pass on their knowledge to someone who is just starting out in to the world of Sass.

As an aside, you will see similar guidelines on the Sass site, at `http://sass-lang.com/community-guidelines`.

Summary

The discovery and exploring of a technology for the first time can open up some real possibilities – this particularly applies to the world of Sass! We've covered some useful tips and tricks in the first part of our voyage through Sass, so let's take a moment to recap what we've learned.

We kicked off with an introduction to Sass as a technology, exploring what it is, and the reasons why we might want to use it in our projects. We then covered some of the different versions and syntaxes associated with Sass, before making sure we were clear on the one we'll use in this book.

Next up came the initial installation of Sass; we saw how easy it was to compile our first file, before exploring what happens during the compilation process. We then moved onto looking at setting up a suitable workflow to get the best out of using Sass, before covering how to automate the compilation process, so we can spend time on more important tasks. We then rounded out the chapter with a quick look at some of the key terms we'll cover throughout this book and how to get help, in case we get stuck.

Phew – it's a good start, but there is so much more to cover! In the next chapter we'll begin to really get stuck into using Sass; our first port of call will be to learn how creating variables and mixins can help reduce the amount of code and simplify the process of keeping values updated. All aboard folks – the ship is about to depart...

CHAPTER 2

Introducing Variables and Mixins

It's late on Friday, you've had a busy week and are looking forward to finishing up for the day. In your mind, you can see a welcoming cold drink with your name all over it, waiting for you at home ... except your boss enters the office, and judging by the look on his face, any thought of finishing on time is rapidly disappearing out the window. ...

I'll bet this scenario sounds all too familiar: customers who – shall we say, are challenging? – aren't happy with a design, and want to try changing the color scheme. However, their site is really complicated, with different colors in use throughout the style sheet. Sure, you can do a search and replace, but do you really want to have to wade through thousands of lines of code to make sure you've changed all of the colors ...?

Creating Variables in a Practical Context

Absolutely not! There is indeed a better way to do this – enter the power of Sass. One of the key features of Sass is variables; they work in the same way as many scripting languages, such as JavaScript. Now – before you run screaming to the hills: don't worry – it's not as complicated as it sounds. Let me explain how this works, using colors as the basis for our example.

© Alex Libby 2019
A. Libby, *Introducing Dart Sass*, https://doi.org/10.1007/978-1-4842-4372-5_2

When working in a style sheet, normal practice would be to assign colors where needed throughout our style sheet – if we had to change them, we'd likely perform a search and replace. There's nothing wrong with this, provided we've used the same case throughout – clearly replacing #fff with #000 won't catch any instance where we've used white instead!

Instead, we can simply set placeholder names for each instance of a color, such as darkGrey or antiqueWhite – for now, it doesn't matter what names are provided (although I will revisit this later) .

The real magic comes at the start of our style sheet – we specify values for each of these placeholders, rather like a legend for a chart. At the point of compiling our code, Sass simply does a search and replace for each instance of our placeholder variable and replaces them with the appropriate value from our "legend" list. It means that if we do have a demanding customer, then we only have one change to make per color – we can change it at the start of our style sheet, and Sass will automatically update it during compilation.

To see how easy it is, let's take a look at a simple example – in our next exercise, we're going to add some simple elements on a page but use variables to apply colors using Sass. I've used colors that work better in a black and white environment (for printing), but this will work with any color you choose.

ASSIGNING VARIABLES

Let's make a start on our code:

1. We'll start by downloading and extracting a copy of the variables folder from the code download that accompanies this book – go ahead and save this folder into our project area.

2. Next, fire up your text editor – we can now add in our styles, so for this, go ahead and create a new file, saving it as variables. scss in the scss subfolder of the variables folder.

3. We'll be adding in a number of styles to our style sheet – the first group is a set of variables we'll use to define colors in this demo:

```
$color-gainsboro: #c0c0c0;
$color-dimgrey: #696969;
$color-slategrey: #708090;
```

4. Leave a bank line, then add the following base styles:

```
@font-face {  font-family: 'pt_sansregular'; src:
url('../font/pt_sansregular.woff') format('woff'); font-
weight: normal; font-style: normal; }
body {  font-family: 'pt_sansregular', sans-serif;
padding: 20px; }
h2 { text-align: center; }
section { border: 1px solid #000; width: 450px; padding:
20px; margin-left: auto; margin-right: auto; }
```

5. Leave another blank line, then immediately below add in the following styles that will make use of Sass:

```
section span { color: $color-dimgrey; font-size: 20px;
font-weight: bold; }
p { color: $color-gainsboro; font-size: 16px; font-
weight: bold;}
a { color: $color-slategrey; text-decoration: none; }
a:hover { text-decoration: underline; background-color:
antiquewhite; font-weight: bold; }
```

6. Save the file as variables.scss in the scss folder.

7. Next, fire up a terminal session and change the working folder to the variables folder under our project area.

8. At the prompt, type the following command and press Enter:

    ```
    sass sass\variables.scss css\variables.css
    ```

9. If all is well, we should see a `variables.css` file appear
    in the `css` folder, along with a source map – previewing
    the results will show a simple box with styled elements, as
    indicated in Figure 2-1.

Introducing Sass: Creating Variables

A title set to 20px height

A paragraph

A link to Apress.com

Figure 2-1. *Creating basic variables*

See how easy that was? Granted, our example was very simplistic, but
this doesn't matter – we can use this in all types of different scenarios. This
is an important feature to come to grips with, so let's take a few moments
to understand how this works in greater detail.

Exploring What Happened

Although the idea of using variables may scare some, creating and using
variables isn't as hard as it might look. We touched on this in our first
demo back in Chapter 1, when we compiled a single style rule that used
three variables.

In reality, using variables is nothing more than a search and replace –
our demo made use of three variables, namely $color-gainsboro, $color-
dimgrey, and $color-slategrey. To each of these, we assign the relevant
color code (we could use RGB, or even RGBA if we'd wanted). We then
added the appropriate variable at the appropriate point in our code – so,

for example $color-gainsboro appears against the color attribute at line 22. At the point of compilation, Sass looks for each variable used and simply replaces them with the appropriate value – in this instance, our value would become color: #c0c0c0; in the compiled style sheet.

To prove this is the case, take a look at the compiled style sheet from within your browser's DOM inspector – if we have source map support enabled, we'll see the final compiled result, along with a link to the original source file, as indicated in Figure 2-2.

```
section span {                          variables.scss:31
    color: ▉#696969;
    font-size: 20px;
    font-weight: bold;
}
```

Figure 2-2. *Viewing compiled CSS in a browser*

If we were to click on the variables.scss name shown in Figure 2-2, we'd see the original Sass code, as shown in Figure 2-3.

```
31  section span {
32      color: $color-dimgrey;
33      font-size: 20px;
34      font-weight: bold;
35  }
```

Figure 2-3. *Translating compiled CSS to original SCSS*

At this point, there are a couple of points we should be aware of: our naming convention, and making sure we use the right names! This is something that could easily trip you up, so let's take a moment to cover this in more detail.

Taking Care Over Variable Names

Names, names – surely all we need is something to identify a value, right ...?

Well, yes – and no. Sure, any name we give must give some indication of what it relates to, but there is more to it than that when using Sass. Let me explain what I mean:

In our example, we've used the format `$color-XXXXX` to name three colors. By themselves, they seem reasonable: there's something of a naming convention in place, and the format is consistent.

But – I'm sure we know what `dimgrey` is as a color: Could you tell what `gainsboro` is though? All three colors are various shades of gray; however, what indication do we have that this is the case? None – to get around this, there are a couple of changes we can consider making:

- When creating colors, consider reordering the names used, so instead of `$color-dimgrey`, have something such as `$grey-dim`, or `$grey-dark`. This makes the name more modular – we're sharing common terms, and describing their function means we're going from generic to specific, in much the same way as CSS works with specificity.

- We can take it a step further though – instead of putting the color directly into our Sass rules, we can create a variable to describe the color according to its function in our code. When it comes to editing, most editors will automatically display suggested colors, based on what we've defined in our variable list. So, to rewrite our previous example, it would look something like this:

```
$grey-dim: #696969;

$color-title: $grey-dim;

section span { color: $color-title; font-size: 20px;
font-weight: bold; }
```

- It has the added bonus that if we decide to change the shade of color for $color-title, then we can do this in one go: we only need to change one entry, rather than change multiple entries throughout our code.

There is not necessarily any right or wrong way to write variables, particularly where colors are involved; it makes sense, though, to ensure you use a consistent naming convention. Making it modular, as we have done here, means that we can even define a small palette of colors and use functions to create completely different colors!

To see what I mean, check out the examples by Jackie Balzer at http://jackiebalzer.com/color – all of them have been created from just one color - #f8af1e, or a deep shade of yellow. We'll revisit this idea in Chapter 4, "Calculating Values Using Observations."

There is a more serious side though to using variables – when writing code for this book, I came across the compilation error shown in Figure 2-4.

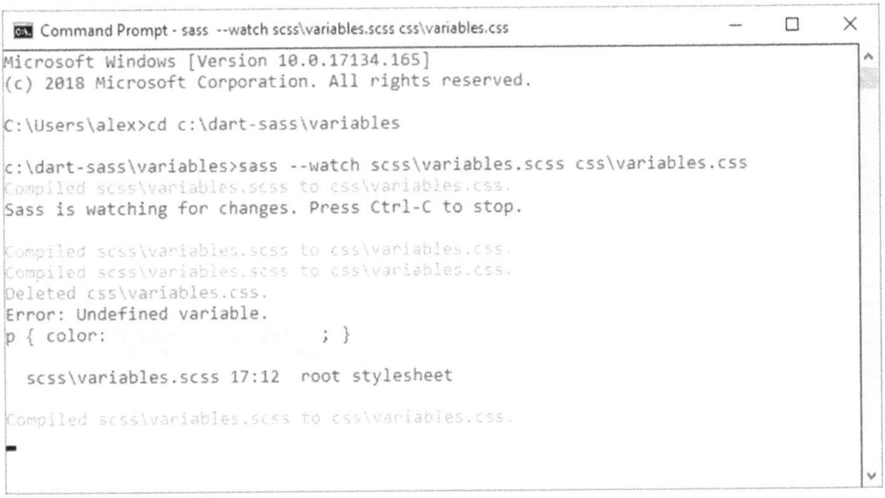

Figure 2-4. Dealing with a compilation error

At first glance it looks a little blunt, but in reality, there is a simple cause.

In this example, I had used the `--watch` parameter to automatically compile the code when changes were made. However, the colors used in the demo weren't suitable; I had to change them. I'd removed the `$color-antiqueyellow` variable but not updated a rule that still referred to this variable. Sass quite rightly complained – the fix, of course, is to make sure the style rule is updated.

In this case, if we had used the example we covered at the start of this section, then potentially we could avoid generating the error – as long as we don't remove one of the other variables too! Variables make managing code much easier, but it does pay to take care over the use of a naming convention, and how your code is updated during development.

Adding Comments

Up until now, we've written very simple CSS rules – the rule name should be reasonably self-explanatory as to how it might be used. Trouble is, what happens if we start to add more and more rules, particularly if some of those rules aren't as self-explanatory?

Clearly, we need comments – thankfully Sass supports them in much the same way as we would use them in CSS. There are a couple of things we need to be aware of though:

- If we use single line comments, these will be removed by default at compilation;

- If we use multi-line comments, these will be removed if the output style is set to compressed, but left untouched when set to expanded.

To see what I mean, let's dive in and put this to the test.

COMPILING COMMENTS

1. Go ahead and open up one of the Sass files from a previous demo – I've used the one from the variables folder.

2. Add the following code as highlighted, then save the file:

```
/* This is a test comment
 * over several lines, which
 * uses the standard CSS comment
 * syntax, and will appear in
 * compiled output */
```

```
$color-gainsboro: #c0c0c0;
```

3. Next, fire up a terminal session and change the working folder to the variables folder under our project area.

4. At the prompt, type the following command and press Enter:

```
sass sass\variables.scss css\variables.css
```

5. If all is well, we should see a variables.css and source map files appear in the css folder as before – if you open it up this time though, you will see the comment appear at the start of our style sheet (Figure 2-5).

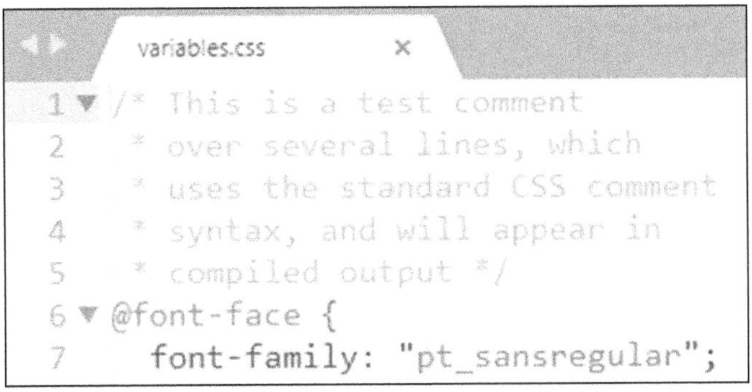

Figure 2-5. *The results of compiling with comments*

6. Try running the compile command, but this time with a slight change:

```
sass --style=compressed sass\variables.scss css\
variables.css
```

If we take a look at the compiled file, notice how it has disappeared?

7. This time, try replacing the multi-line comment with this single line one:

// This is a test comment

```
@font-face {
```

8. Try compiling the code now – notice how the comment is removed, and that if you run the compilation again with `style=compressed` attribute set, the comment is still removed.

See how easy it is to manage comments? Adding comments is an important part of writing a style sheet; the key point though is that we should be careful about which style of comment to use, so that we strike the right balance between adding comments throughout our source, and those that remain in our compiled style sheet. Okay - time for us to change tack: let's take a look at our next feature in Sass. How many times have you written code that could be reusable, with or without tweaking it?

Making Use of Standard Mixins

If you spend time writing CSS, I am sure you will come across occasions where it can get a little tedious - creating font styles, animating using `transform`, scalable elements such as videos, dealing with vendor prefixes (where they still apply), and the like.

To remove some of this tedium, we can make use of a great feature in Sass: mixins. These allow us to group together CSS declarations into blocks of code that we can reuse throughout our projects. We can use one of two types – basic mixins are simply slotted into our code, whereas parametric mixins allow us to pass in values, but still use the same core styles. We'll cover how these work shortly, but let's first take a look at implement reusable code, with basic mixins.

Creating Reusable Code

We touched on a couple of use case scenarios in our introduction, where mixins would be a perfect solution – one in particular is to center responsive content on the page, no matter how it is scaled.

When creating responsive content, we would typically use percentage values – Chris Coyier of CSS-Tricks.com came up with a great mixin that allows us to center any content, leaving us free to style it as we wish. I've used this as a basis for our next demo, which will center a standard `<div>` element on screen.

You can see Chris's original example at `https://codepen.io/chriscoyier/pen/BvdgL`.

CREATING MIXINS

Let's make a start on that code:

1. We'll begin by downloading and extracting a copy of the `centerdiv` folder to our project area.

2. In your usual text editor, go ahead and create a new document, then add in the following lines of code – we'll begin with a variable followed by our mixin:

```
$color-slategrey: #708090;

@mixin centerdiv { position: absolute; left: 50%; top:
50%; transform: translate(-50%, -50%); }
```

3. Leave a blank line, then add in the following base styles for our demo:

```
@font-face { font-family: 'pt_sansregular'; src: url('../
font/pt_sansregular.woff') format('woff'); font-weight:
normal; font-style: normal; }

body { font-family: 'pt_sansregular', sans-serif;
background: #fff; }

h2 { text-align: center; }
```

4. We've added in our mixin, but it won't be used unless we make a call to it – for this, add the following style rule below the previous set of rules:

```
div {
  @include centerdiv;

  width: 40%; height: 50%; padding: 20px; background:
  $color-slategrey; color: antiquewhite; text-align:
  center; box-shadow: 0 0 30px rgba(0, 0, 0, 0.2);
  border-radius: 10px; font-size: 18px; font-weight:
  bold; letter-spacing: 1px;
}
```

5. Save this file as centerdiv.scss in the scss subfolder within the centerdiv folder we saved in step 1.

6. Next, fire up a terminal session and change the working folder to the centerdiv folder under our project area. At the prompt, enter the following command and press Enter:

```
sass sass\centerdiv.scss css\centerdiv.css
```

7. If all is well, we should see a `centerdiv.css` file appear in the `css` folder, along with a source map – previewing the results will show a simple box that remains centered on screen, as indicated in Figure 2-6.

Introducing Sass: Creating a Simple Mixin

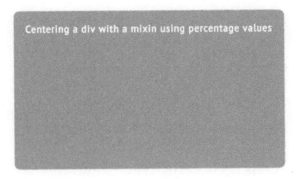

Centering a div with a mixin using percentage values

Figure 2-6. *Centering a div using a mixin*

Try resizing your browser window – notice that no matter how small or large you make it, the div element is always centered on screen? Although we've set suitable values for left and top in our code, they won't work by themselves – let's quickly cover what really makes this demo come together.

Exploring Our Code in Detail

The test of our demo lies in how our Sass code has been compiled – we can see the first part of it in Figure 2-7.

```
div {                                          centerdiv.scss:26
    position: absolute;
    left: 50%;
    top: 50%;
    transform: translate(-50%, -50%);
    width: 40%;
    height: 50%;
    padding: ▶ 20px;
    background: ▶ ■#708090;
    color: □antiquewhite;
    text-align: center;
    box-shadow: ▢0 0 30px ■rgba(0, 0, 0, 0.2);
    border-radius: ▶ 10px;
    font-size: 18px;
    font-weight: bold;
    letter-spacing: 1px;
}
```

Figure 2-7. *Our mixin, compiled as CSS*

Our demo incorporated the contents of the centerdiv mixin during compilation – mixins are written as CSS rules but must be proceeded with the keyword @mixin and referenced using the keyword @include with the mixin name.

The key thing to note is that mixins will not themselves be compiled, but the rules within will be included into any ruleset that calls the mixin. It does mean that our source file may be larger than the compiled version, but this doesn't matter: as long as we create suitable mixins, they will only be included in rulesets that call them, and not be compiled themselves in our style sheet.

Using Prebuilt Mixins

Armed with our newfound knowledge of creating mixins, we can go ahead and create new ones for use in our projects. However, before we go and reinvent the wheel, why not take a look online?

A look on Google will show dozens of people who have written mixins and released them for use; more often than not, we may find someone who has written a mixin already that would serve our needs. Using existing mixins will save us time and development effort – granted, we may have to tweak the code, but it will remove the need to develop something from scratch.

USING PREBUILT MIXINS

There are dozens of mixins available online, either single or as part of libraries – if you search on Google for "sass mixin libraries," you will see references to the likes of Bourbon, Scotch, and Compass, among others. Some of these have been around for some time; with the advances of CSS, they become less and less useful (primarily if they contain vender-prefixed versions of code that are no longer necessary) .

One example of a mixin library is CSSgram, created by Una Kravets – this is a take on the filters used in the popular Instagram applet. Available from `https://una.im/CSSgram/`, we're going to make use of one of the filters to style a before and after of a vintage image.

For this demo, we'll be using the image of a camera from `https://www.pexels.com/photo/camera-photography-vintage-old-36732/`; please feel free to adjust if you want to use another image.

Let's start creating our demo:

1. We'll begin by downloading and extracting a copy of the `prebuilt` folder to our project area.

2. In your usual text editor, go ahead and create a new document, then add in the following lines of code – we'll begin some base styles for our demo:

49

```scss
@import "cssgram.scss";

@font-face { font-family: 'pt_sansregular'; src: url('../
font/pt_sansregular.woff') format('woff'); font-weight:
normal; font-style: normal; }

body { font-family: 'pt_sansregular', sans-serif;
background: #fff; }

h2 { text-align: center; }
```

3. We now need to add in the styles that will place the images on the page:

```scss
p { width: 100px; display: inline-block; margin: 0;
padding: 0; }

section { width: 320px; margin-left: auto; margin-right:
auto; }

div.filter, div.nofilter { width: 300px; display: inline-
block; margin: 10px; }
```

4. Last but by no means least come the styles required to implement the filter used in our demo:

```scss
div.filter { @extend %stinson; }

div.nofilter img { width: 100%; z-index: 1; }
```

5. Save this file as `prebuilt.scss` in the `scss` subfolder within the `prebuilt` folder we saved in step 1.

6. Next, fire up a terminal session and change the working folder to the `prebuilt` folder under our project area. At the prompt enter the following command and press Enter:

```
sass sass\prebuilt.scss css\prebuilt.css
```

7. If all is well, we should see a `prebuilt.css` file appear in the `css` folder, along with a source map – previewing the results will show two images, one without a filter and one with, as indicated in Figure 2-8.

Introducing SASS: Using Prebuilt Mixins

Before:

After:

Figure 2-8. *Applying a filter using a mixin library*

Although our demo is relatively straightforward to create, there is a key point that deserves further attention. If you take a look at the CSSgram file download, you'll see it is huge. It is full of different filter effects – it would be understandable if you had become concerned at just how much code we're using! Fortunately, we're using a lot less than it would initially appear – let's dive in and take a look in more detail.

Understanding How the Code Works

So – even though we're making use of the CSSgram mixin library, how come our CSS style sheet isn't larger than it should be?

The trick behind making this work is the use of the `@import` statement at the head of our style sheet – by default, Sass only imports mixins *where there is a direct reference* to them from within our code. In this case we've only called the `stinson` mixin, so Sass simply ignores all of the other filter mixin files in the `scss` folder during compilation.

Including the file extension is not obligatory when importing files: in this instance, we could use `@import "cssgram";` equally as well in our demo. We'll touch on this later in this chapter.

However, there is a twist in this tale: the keen-eyed among you should spot that our code doesn't include the mixin keyword! What gives? Well, we're making use of another feature: `@extend`. We'll cover this in more detail in Chapter 3, "Creating Nesting Styles," but for now, it's enough to know that it works in a similar fashion to mixins but can produce more efficient code.

If you take a look at the `stinson.scss` file, though, you will indeed see the `@include` keyword in use; this calls a base filter mixin, which is used in all of the filters within the CSSgram library. There are some key differences though to how mixins and the `@extend` keyword work; we'll explore this in more detail, when we take a look at using `@extend` in the next chapter.

Okay – let's move on: creating or importing base mixins is a great way to write more efficient code, but there is one small limitation. There will come a point where you may have multiple blocks of code that could be served by a single mixin, but different values are needed. Ordinarily we might think there isn't anything we can do, but as we're using Sass, there is – it's time to learn about parametric mixins.

Passing Values to Mixins

So far, we've explored how to create and use mixins – these are perfect for including reusable, static groups of rules, but what if we had instances where we could use a mixin but can't as values are not quite the same?

There may be occasions where we might be able to fine tweak values so that we can, but this is unlikely – a far better idea is to make use of parametric mixins. These work in much the same way as standard mixins, but with one difference – instead of containing a static set of values, we can pass different values into the mixin and allow Sass to render it as standard CSS.

The syntax for parametric mixins is very similar – we have the same @mixin keyword at the start, but this time around we include the values we'll be passing into the mixin:

```
@mixin button-bg($bg, $fg) {

...the values are used in the mixin...

}
```

At the point of compilation, Sass inserts the different values into the placeholders within the mixin and compiles it into valid CSS, ready for use in our projects. We can see how this works in more detail, by creating a demo around the humble button – we often have different colors in use in a site, so this makes it a perfect fit for using mixins.

CREATING PARAMETRIC MIXINS

Let's start creating our demo:

1. We'll begin by downloading and extracting a copy of the parametric folder to our project area.

2. In your usual text editor, go ahead and create a new document, then add in the following lines of code – we'll begin some base styles for our demo:

```
@mixin button-bg($bg, $fg) {
  background: $bg;
  color: $fg;
  &:hover {
    background:darken($bg,8%);
    transition: all 0.3s ease;
  }
  &:active {
    background:darken($bg,30%);
  }
}

@font-face { font-family: 'pt_sansregular'; src: url('../
font/pt_sansregular.woff') format('woff'); font-weight:
normal; font-style: normal; }

body { font-family: 'pt_sansregular', sans-serif;
padding: 20px;}

h2 { text-align: center; }

p { margin: 0; padding: 0; margin-bottom: 30px; width:
480px; margin-left: auto; margin-right: auto;
```

3. We now need to add in the styles that will place the buttons on the page:

```
.wrap { margin:0 auto; width: 800px; text-align:center; }

.btn { text-decoration: none; padding: 5px 10px; border-
radius: 4px; font-size: 22px; }
```

4. We've added the base style for our button, but for them to resemble something useful, we need to provide some color. The following rules will take care of this:

```
.btn-antiquewhite { @include button-bg(#faebd7, #000); }
.btn-darkgrey { @include button-bg(#a9a9a9, #000); }
.btn-gainsboro{ @include button-bg(#dcdcdc, #000); }
.btn-slategrey { @include button-bg(#708090, #fff); }
```

5. Save this file as `parametric.scss` in the `scss` subfolder within the `parametric` folder we saved in step 1.

6. Next, fire up a terminal session and change the working folder to the `parametric` folder under our project area. At the prompt, enter the following command and press Enter:

```
sass sass\parametric.scss css\parametric.css
```

7. If all is well, we should see a `parametric.css` file appear in the `css` folder (in the same way as previous exercises), along with a source map – previewing the results will show a series of styled buttons, as indicated in Figure 2-9.

Introducing Sass: Creating Buttons

Use SASS to detect your background colors and other styles and apply them to your buttons for consistent global hovers and active states.

Figure 2-9. *Creating buttons with parametric mixins*

This demo may be simple, but it is a perfect way to illustrate the effectiveness of using parametric mixins. We've created four different buttons using the same base code but with different values passed in – let's take a look at how this works in practice.

55

Dissecting Our Code

So – how does our demo manage to produce four identically shaped buttons, yet with different colors for each one? The trick to making our demo work lies in this mixin:

```
@mixin button-bg($bg, $fg) {
  background: $bg;
  color: $fg;
  &:hover {
    background:darken($bg,8%);
    transition: all 0.3s ease;
  }
  &:active {
    background:darken($bg,30%);
  }
}
```

By itself, it won't do anything, but once we call it from within our code, it will compile into the styles required for each button. If we take the first call as an example:

```
.btn-antiquewhite { @include button-bg(#faebd7, #000); }
```

… we see that the first value passed in is #faebd7; this represents an off-white (or antique) shade of white. The second value passed into our mixin is black – this will be used to style the text shown in our button.

When we look at the hover function, this is where it gets interesting – we have several new keywords in use. It starts with the use of &: - this is a reference to the parent selector, so when compiled, it becomes .btn-antiquewhite:hover. We then use the $bg variable (represents the first value passed to our mixin) and the Sass darken() function to produce two new colors: #f5d9b3 for the hover state, and #e9a74f for our button's active state.

We'll revisit references to parent selectors as part of nesting, in the next chapter.

Okay – let's move on: we're almost ready to start looking at a new part of Sass, but before we do so, we need to revisit a feature we've touched on earlier in this chapter. Managing Sass style sheets can get tricky, the larger they grow. The question is how to best manage them before they do get too unwieldy?

Working Across Multiple Files

Over the course of this chapter, we've created simple style sheets – these work well, but as we've just mentioned, they can cause real problems if they get too large!

Thankfully we can make use of Sass's `@import` option to help break down our style sheet into smaller, more manageable chunks. This function already exists within standard CSS, but Sass extends its functionality. We touched on how to use it back in the "Using prebuilt mixins" demo; as a quick reminder, we can create any number of Sass files, which contain variables, mixins, and the like:

```
// _reset.scss

html, body, ul, ol { margin:  0; padding: 0; }
```

We then import them into our style sheet as needed, as indicated in this example:

```
// base.scss

@import 'reset';

body { font: 100% Helvetica, sans-serif; background-color: #efefef; }
```

Notice how in our base.scss example file, we're not specifying a file extension? These are not obligatory; Sass will look for files that end in either .sass (the old format), or .scss (the current format) and import them accordingly. In this case, our code example would compile to this:

```
html, body, ul, ol { margin: 0; padding: 0; }
body { font: 100% Helvetica, sans-serif; background-color:
#efefef; }
```

This gives us a perfect excuse to group styles together in separate files, such as variables, font mixins, resets, and so on – we can then import them as needed into our project.

To learn more about importing, please refer to the documentation on the Dart Sass site at http://sass-lang.com/documentation/ file.SASS_REFERENCE.html#import.

In our next demo, we'll put this to the test by converting our previous buttons demo to use an imported file – you'll see how easy it is to make the switch!

IMPORTING FILES

Let's make a start on updating the previous demo:

1. We'll begin by downloading and extracting a copy of the import folder and saving it to our project area.

2. We need to extract the mixin from our main Sass file and move it to a new one – for this, go ahead and create a new file called mixins.scss; store this in the scss subfolder within the import folder. Leave it open for the moment, as we will use it in the next step.

3. Go ahead and open `importfile.scss` in your text editor, then copy lines 1 to 11 and paste them in `mixins.scss`. Save the file, and close it.

4. Revert back to `importfile.scss`, then delete lines 1 to 11. Add in the following line of code, as highlighted:

@import "mixins";

```
@font-face {
    font-family: 'pt_sansregular';
    src: url('../font/pt_sansregular.woff') format('woff');
```

5. Save `inportfile.scss` and close it – we can now compile the file to produce our style sheet.

6. Next, fire up a terminal session and change the working folder to the import folder under our project area. At the prompt, type the following command and press Enter:

```
sass sass\importfile.scss css\importfile.css
```

7. If all is well, we should see a importfile.css file appear in the css folder (in the same way as previous exercises), along with a source map – previewing the results will show the same set of styled buttons from before, as indicated in Figure 2-10.

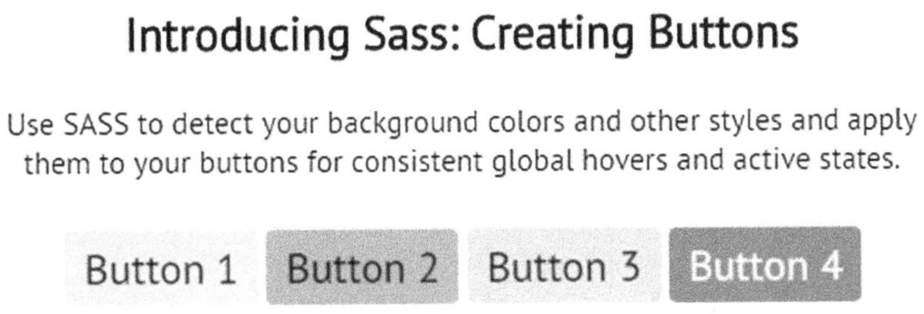

Introducing Sass: Creating Buttons

Use SASS to detect your background colors and other styles and apply them to your buttons for consistent global hovers and active states.

Button 1   Button 2   Button 3   Button 4

Figure 2-10. Our (updated) styled buttons

This is an easy way to improve the management of our style sheet – the trick though is to learn how best to manage the breakdown of files into smaller ones, so that we don't end up importing files unnecessarily! There are a couple of useful tips around importing files that we should be aware of, so let's take a look at them in more detail.

Exploring How Our Code Works

Although we've had to make a few changes to our code, this relatively straightforward change can be a real life saver! Take, for example, a standard style sheet for a CMS application such as WordPress – its' style sheet weighs into some 4,500+ lines, so the ability to break down our styles into smaller files is a real boon.

Focusing on our demo, we've moved the existing button-bg mixin into a new file, and removed it from the original master file. The original lines in the master file were replaced with an appropriately named @import statement, which calls the file in during compilation. Sass then merges the content into one file and produces one finished style sheet at the end of the compilation process. If we wanted to, we can verify that the code is indeed coming from two separate files, as indicated in Figure 2-11.

```
element.style {
}
.btn-slategrey:hover {                    mixins.scss:4
    background: ▶ ■#5e6c79;
    transition: ▶ all 0.3s ▨ease;
}
.btn-slategrey {                          importfile.scss:54
    background: ▶ ■#708090;
    color: ☐#fff;
}
.btn {                                    importfile.scss:34
```

Figure 2-11. *Proving our mixin file is being used ...*

It does raise some important questions though about managing imported files – the aforementioned WordPress file isn't one long style sheet but is made up from multiple imported files. It means that we can use one to store variables, another to deal with the header, a third for posts, and perhaps a fourth for responsive media queries, and so on. The real trick is to make sure that we store the right content in each file, so that we're not importing files that then import others – that can become really messy if we're not careful!

In addition, there are some occasions though where imported files will not be compiled as a Sass file, but as a CSS file – they are:

- If the file's extension is .css

- If the filename begins with http://

- If the filename is a url()

- If the @import has any media queries

Provided the extension ends in `.scss` (or `.sass`) then Sass will attempt to import the file into the master style sheet during the compilation process.

61

Summary

Phew – that was a bit of a whistle-stop tour through Sass variables and mixins! We've covered some useful key topics throughout this chapter, so let's take a moment to review what we've learned.

We kicked off our journey through the world of Sass with a look first at creating variables; we covered how these can be really useful to implement, particularly when working with values such as colors. We explored how it pays to take care over our choice of names, so that if changes are needed, then we can reduce the impact of those changes to our code.

Next up came a quick exploration of adding comments – we saw how these in the main are similar to standard CSS, but that there are some differences when compiling Sass code.

We then moved onto learning about mixins – we started with creating a basic mixin, before learning how to incorporate mixins created by others, and taking a look at ones that can produce different code based on values passed into the mixin. We then rounded out the chapter by revisiting the subject of importing separate files into our Sass development, so we can better manage our code during development.

We won't be stopping for long though – we still have plenty to cover! We've created single rules, but there are often occasions where some of the rules we create are duplicated in part (as they touch the same element, class or selector ID). This can make developing styles repetitive – what if we could nest our styles, or reuse existing styles more efficiently? We can – you'll learn all you need to started in the next chapter.

CHAPTER 3

Creating Nested Styles

If you spend any time writing CSS styles, I have no doubt that sooner or later, you will have come across instances where your code contains selectors or classes that go several levels deep. What do I mean by this? Well, let me explain.

Take, for example, a navigation bar. This has been around for years – it's a basic staple of websites, although how we decide to skin it will differ between sites. However, the basic principle uses unordered lists, which can go several levels deep:

```
<nav>
  <li>
    <a href="#">Heading 1</a>
      <ul>
        <li><a href="#">Test link</a></li>
        <li><a href="#">Test link </a></li>
        <li><a href="#">Test link</a></li>
        <li><a href="#">Test link</a></li>
      </ul>
  </li>
```

© Alex Libby 2019
A. Libby, *Introducing Dart Sass*, https://doi.org/10.1007/978-1-4842-4372-5_3

```
<li><a href="#">Heading 2</a></li>
<li>
  <a href="#">Heading 3</a>
  <ul>
    <li><a href="#">Test link</a></li>
    <li><a href="#">Test link</a></li>
    <li><a href="#">Test link</a></li>
    <li><a href="#">Test link</a></li>
  </ul>
</li>
</nav>
```

Granted, our example is a little simplistic, but hopefully you get the idea! To style our example, we would use the following classes:

```
nav {...}
nav li a {...}
nav li ul {...}
nav li ul li a {...}
```

Notice any similarities between each style – say, for example, how some of the element names repeat themselves ...?

The elements we're using are fairly short, but if we had decided to reference longer class names (such as ul.navigation li a.about ul li a, for example), then our code will soon become awkward to read. This will cause a real problem – is there a better way? Thankfully, with the power of Sass there is – let me introduce you to the concept of nesting.

Breaking Apart the Concept of Nesting

Put simply, nesting allows us to store (or nest) styles within others, when there is a clear sense of commonality between elements. This means that instead of having to write the class or selector out in full for each rule, we can just include the part is specific to our nested rule. At the point of compilation, Sass will turn each declaration into a valid rule by referencing the parent selector or class. To see what I mean, let's take our simple example and convert it to Sass:

```
nav {
  ...
  li {
    a {...}
    ul {...}
    li a {...}
  }
}
```

There – that looks a little easier to read, right? Nesting is a great time saver, as it helps cut down the number of times we have to repeat the same selector; it also feels more natural and easier to understand when reading our code.

Let's put this into practice and create – yes, you probably guessed what's coming: a basic navigation! Nesting can be used at any time when developing Sass – as long as we have multiple styles that reference the same parent element or class, then nesting can be applied. As it so happens, navigation lends itself really well to nesting, so let's dive in and see how this works in practice.

CREATING A SIMPLE MENU BAR

Let's make a start on creating our demo:

1. We'll begin by downloading and extracting a copy of the nesting folder from the code download that accompanies this book – save it to our project area.

2. Next, fire up your text editor – we're going to add in the styles needed for our demo.

3. We'll add the code required, in blocks – go ahead and add the following base styles for our demo:

```
@font-face {
  font-family: 'pt_sansregular';
  src: url('../font/pt_sansregular.woff') format('woff');
  font-weight: normal;
  font-style: normal;
}

body {
  font-family: 'pt_sansregular', sans-serif;
  padding: 20px;
}

h1 {
  font-size: 20px;
}
```

4. The crux of our demo is the navigation bar we're creating – for this, add the following style rule below the previous h1 tag, leaving a blank line after that tag:

```
nav {
  width: 600px;
}
```

5. Next, we need to add in the style rule for our unordered list that forms our navigation – for this, leave a blank line after the width: 600px declaration, then add this:

```
ul {
  list-style: none;
  margin: 0 3%;
  padding: 0;
}
```

6. With our unordered list container in place, we can now style each of the menu items – for this, leave a blank line after the closing bracket of the previous step, then add this:

```
li {
  display: inline-block;
  padding-right: 10px;
}
```

7. To make our navigation work, we need to add links for each entry – go ahead and leave a blank line after the closing bracket of step 6, then add these styles:

```
a {
  background-color: #faebd7;
  border: 1px solid #ccc;
  color: #666;
  display: block;
  padding: 6px 12px;
  text-decoration: none;
  font-size: 32px;
}

a:hover, a:focus{
  background-color: darken(#faebd7, 20%);
}

a:active {
  background-color: #666;
  border-color: #666;
  color: #efefef;
}
```

8. Save the file as nesting.scss in the scss folder.

9. Next, fire up a terminal session and change the working folder to the nesting folder under our project area.

10. At the prompt, type the following command and press Enter:

```
sass sass\nesting.scss css\nesting.css
```

11. If all is well, we should see a nesting.css file appear in the css folder, along with a source map.

12. If we preview the results in a browser, we will show a simple box with styled elements, as indicated in Figure 3-1:

Introducing Sass: Creating a Menu using Nesting

This is a basic navigation structure created using Sass' nesting function:

Figure 3-1. *Creating a basic menu using nesting*

See how easy it was to nest our code? The basic principle of nesting is straightforward, but the real test of applying nesting comes with making sure you use the right parent selector, so that any nested style names are as short as possible and keep duplication to a minimum. To see what I mean, let's take a few moments to explore our demo's code in more detail, so you can see how we arrived at the structure used in the code.

Breaking Apart Our Code

Okay, granted, I may have been a little too presumptuous with the beginning statement of that last paragraph, but in reality, nesting isn't a hard technique to understand. The skill lies in making sure that we pick the right selector to form the basis for our nesting. Let's work through our example in a little more detail:

We kicked off this demo by setting some styles to help with the presentation of our demo – the crux of our demo kicks in with the initial <nav> statement on line 17. Any styles we need to apply to the <nav> element sit immediately under it; styles for child rules are then simply indented below this initial declaration. In our case, this means that the ul, li, and a (and pseudo-its classes), are all indented at the first level only. They will become nav ul, nav li, nav a, and so on – Sass understanding that nav in this instance is the common element and therefore acts as the parent.

Working a More Complex Example

Our previous example was hosted at the first level (or indent) – in many cases this may work for your projects, but what if we needed to go a level lower (as we had more subclasses to contend with)?

Well, we can nest more deeply using Sass, although a word of caution – a good rule of thumb is to nest no more than two or three levels deep. Anything else is technically possible, but I would not recommend it – the level of CSS specificity will be too deep, and a good indicator that we should revisit how our style class names are structured.

Assuming we're nesting to sensible levels, then this is an example of how a nested block of code to three levels might work:

```
.sidebar {
  position: fixed;
  height: 100%;

  &-list {
    background-color: white;

    &-link {
      text-decoration: none;
    }
  }
}
```

In this case, the common element is .sidebar; all three styles use this in their names. However, I see an ampersand and hyphen at the start of two of the names – what's that all about? These are **placeholders** – in this instance, the second- and third-level class names will become `.sidebar-list` and `.sidebar-list-link` respectively.

We'll cover placeholders in this context in a little more detail later in this chapter, in "Referencing Parent Selectors."

Okay – to use a common driving expression, it's time to change lanes: nesting is a great technique to learn, but it is not without some quirks. Let's take a look at a few to see what I mean – for now, you may not come across them when starting out with Sass, but sooner or later they may well rear their ugly heads, so to speak ...

Exploring the Pitfalls of Nesting

Take a look at the code example in the previous section again – we mentioned in the previous section that it would create three rules, and Figure 3-2 indeed confirms this is the case.

```
1 ▾ .sidebar {
2       position: fixed;
3       height: 100%;
4
5 ▾     &-list {
6         background-color: white;
7
8 ▾         &-link {
9             text-decoration: none;
10        }
11     }
12 }
13
14
```

```
1 ▾ .sidebar {
2       position: fixed;
3       height: 100%;
4   }
5 ▾ .sidebar-list {
6       background-color: white;
7   }
8 ▾ .sidebar-list-link {
9       text-decoration: none;
10  }
```

Figure 3-2. *Our compiled example, using Sassmeister*

Our code has compiled to valid CSS, producing three example rules from code that is nested to three levels deep. This works very well, but can lead us into a false sense of security! There are advantages and drawbacks to using nesting, if we're not careful, so let's take a look at the downsides first as these are the easiest to explain.

Is Nesting a Bad Thing?

Let's say we're using the following code:

```
<main>
  <div class="one">
    <p class="two">Some text
      <a href=""></a>
    </p>
  </div>
</main>
```

This produces overly specific CSS code – to reference the a tag inside this block of code, we would have to use main.one.two.a as a CSS rule:

```
main {
  .one {
    .two {
      a {color: red}
    }
  }
}
```

This level of specificity is not recommended and should be avoided, as it makes our CSS very tightly coupled to our HTML structure. To override this code, we would have to create even more specific CSS to change this code; this only serves to compound the original problem! What doesn't

71

help is that if you had nested this code using Sass, it would make it appear as if you had styled a simple link. The reality is that Sass just hides the problem, which will still produce the same overly specific code during compilation.

Ultimately, nesting can be a great feature when used with care – as a general rule of thumb, I would recommend using no more than three levels of nesting. This keeps the code simple and easy to read, and it won't produce overly specific code that would otherwise create problems later during development.

Exploring the Benefits of Nesting

Ouch – one might be forgiven for thinking that nesting isn't that great, particularly after that warning! The truth though is that like any tool used responsibly, it can have a very positive impact on your code.

In this instance, the principal benefit of using nesting is in producing code that is easier to read and maintain. Nesting allows us to group all of the child selectors that inherit from a parent together; it also saves on typing, as we don't have to write the parent selector in front of each child selector at the same time. The trick of course is to make sure we don't nest our code too deeply – it may be tempting to go to the extreme, but remember: nesting doesn't fix bad code – if you put rubbish in, then you will only get rubbish out!

Okay – let's move swiftly on: if we're nesting code using Sass, then you might assume that this can cover pseudo-selectors, such as `:hover` and `:focus`, right? Unfortunately not – this will throw an error if you try to nest them in this way. Fortunately there is a solution to this – we need to tweak how we reference them when nesting our code. Let's take a look at what is involved in more detail.

Referencing Parent Selectors

When nesting Sass statements, many will fit in where there is already duplication within our code. However, you will no doubt be using pseudo-selectors of some description in your code – what about these?

Well, Sass can nest them too – instead of simply indenting them in the same way as normal statements, we have to put a placeholder character immediately before the colon. Take for example the extract of code shown in Figure 3-3.

```
a {
    background-color: #faebd7;
    border: 1px solid #ccc;
    color: #666;
    display: block;
    padding: 6px 12px;
    text-decoration: none;
    font-size: 32px;
}

a:hover,
a:focus{
    background-color: darken(#faebd7, 20%);
}
```

Figure 3-3. *Our code, before the update ...*

This shows all three styles (a, a:hover, and a:focus) written out in full – it's perfectly valid code, but is a little wasteful on space, and repeats the selector name. Instead, we can simply nest each style – to show you how this works, we can dive into a quick demo to update the code from the previous menu exercise.

REFERENCING PARENT SELECTORS

Let's see how easy it is to make the change to our code:

1. First, download and extract a copy of the `parent` folder from
   the code download for this book – save this to our project
   folder.

2. Next, open up the `parent.scss` file, and look for these lines,
   on or around line 29:

```
a {
    background-color: #faebd7;
    border: 1px solid #ccc;
    color: #666;
```

3. Go ahead and edit the a rule – we're nesting the `hover` and
   `focus` declarations within it, as indicated in bold:

```
a {
    background-color: #faebd7;
    border: 1px solid #ccc;
    color: #666;
    display: block;
    padding: 6px 12px;
    text-decoration: none;
    font-size: 32px;
        &:hover, &:focus {
            background-color: darken(#faebd7, 20%);
        }
    &:active{ background-color: #666; border-color:
    #666; color: #efefef;    }
}
```

4. Next, go ahead and delete the stand-alone `active`, `hover`, and `focus` rules – we should be left with the ones nested inside the parent a rule, and that the last line of code will be a closing bracket from the nav rule.

5. Save the file as `parent.scss` in the `scss` folder.

6. Next, fire up a terminal session and change the working folder to the `parent` folder under our project area.

7. At the prompt, type the following command and press Enter:

```
sass sass\parent.scss css\parent.css
```

8. If all is well, we should see a `parent.css` file appear in the `css` folder, along with a source map.

9. Try previewing the results in a browser – if all is well, it will show a simple box with styled elements, as indicated in Figure 3-4.

Introducing Sass: Creating a Menu using Nesting

This is a basic navigation structure created using Sass' nesting function:

Figure 3-4. *Updating our navigation demo*

When nesting, this is an important concept to understand – not getting it right, or missing ampersands may at best produce code that is broken (but unlikely to show any errors), or at worst, fail to compile.

The key thing to remember is to include the placeholder – we may not get the right level of nesting immediately, but with the placeholder, the code should at least compile correctly! In the meantime, let's take a quick look at our code in more detail – you will see it uses the same principles as before, with just the addition of the ampersand as a placeholder.

Exploring Our Code in Detail

If we had run a completed version of this demo, without having seen the changes we've made, then you might be forgiven for thinking that it looks no different to the original version of this demo! Don't worry – this is intentional: it shows that although changes have been made to nest some of the classes we've used, the test shows that our demo still runs correctly.

So – what did we change? Well, the changes in this instance are minor – we moved the hover, focus and active pseudo-selectors inside the parent a rule. In each instance, we've inserted an ampersand to tell Sass to reference the parent class when compiling this rule; this will transform it into the same valid CSS we used in the original nesting demo.

Applying the @extend Directive

There are often cases during development, where we might decide that to style an element, we first create a base class, then add subsequent classes to cover variations of the base class. A good example of this would be designing alert messages – our base class would include the styles needed to create the shell, with the variations (in terms of styling, icons) covered by the use of subsequent classes that inherit from the base class.

The trouble is, this approach is not without its problems – it means we have not one but at least two classes in use; this creates a maintenance burden and can be tricky to debug at a later date. Question is: Can we get around this?

Absolutely – let me introduce you to the extend keyword! This keyword takes the following syntax:

```
@extend .classname;
```

... and allows classes to share a set of properties with other classes. To use it, we would specify the name of the extend class as a declaration within a CSS rule, thus:

```
.classname {
  border: 1px solid black;
  font-weight: bold;
}

.foo {
  @extend .classname;
  color: #fcc;

  ...
}
```

In this instance, we will end up with two classes – .foo and .classname - both sharing the same font-weight and border properties. The .foo class will also have the color property set as a separate declaration.

Working Through an Example

Making use of @extend is perfect if we want to reduce the reliance on multiple classes; we can instead create a rule that is inherited by others during compilation.

To see what I mean, take a look at this example piece of code:

```
.error {
  border: 1px #f00;
  background-color: #fdd;
}

.seriousError {
  @extend .error;
  border-width: 3px;
}
```

When compiling (using a tool such as Sassmeister), we get the CSS shown in Figure 3-5.

```
1  .error, .seriousError {
2      border: 1px #f00;
3      background-color: #fdd;
4  }
5
6  .seriousError {
7      border-width: 3px;
8  }
```

Figure 3-5. *The results of compiling an @extend*

See how the second rule (`.seriousError`) has inherited the properties defined in the first rule, as well as kept the property specified in its own rule? This is perfect for styling elements that share the same properties – we write one rule for our base declaration, then use @extend in each class that needs to inherit this rule and specify additional properties unique to that class.

This feature can be a little tricky to get our heads around and fully understand its use, so let's begin with a demo to show off how it works in more detail.

A Practical Example

Cast your minds back – anyone remember Polaroids? Yes, before the advent of digital images, Polaroids were all the rage: no need to wait for films to be developed, when the final picture appeared in just a few minutes, once we had taken the shot!

Polaroid cameras may not be as popular as they once were, but the effect still lives on – it's very easy to re-create the effect of a Polaroid (the image look, not the developing process!). Let's take a look at how, using the power of Sass and its @extend function.

EXTENDING SASS CLASSES

Let's make a start on coding our demo:

1. We'll begin by downloading and extracting a copy of the extend folder from the code download that accompanies this book – go ahead and save the folder to our project folder.

2. Next, go ahead and open your text editor – we have a whole bunch of styles to add to our demo! We'll add them block by block, beginning with some basic styles for our demo:

```
%imgeffect {
  height: 20%;
  width: 47%;
  bottom: 30px;
  right: 12px;
  box-shadow: 0 33.6px 32px rgba(0,0,0,0.4);
}

@font-face {
  font-family: 'pt_sansregular';
  src: url('../font/pt_sansregular.woff') format('woff');
  font-weight: normal;
  font-style: normal;
}

* {
  box-sizing: border-box;
}
```

```
body {
  font-family: 'pt_sansregular', sans-serif;
  margin: 32px;
}
```

3. This next block adds a set of styles common to each of the
    polaroid effect images:

```
.polaroid {
  background: #fff;
  padding: 16px;
  box-shadow: 0 3.2px 19.2px rgba(0,0,0,0.2);
}

.polaroid > img {
  max-width: 100%;
  height: auto;
}

.caption {
  font-size: 28px;
  text-align: center;
  line-height: 32px;
}
```

4. We now need to style each of the images we've added using
    the Polaroid effect – this adds the initial grayscale effect and
    rotates the images off their horizontal position:

```
.item {
  width: 30%;
  display: inline-block;
  filter: grayscale(100%);
}
```

```
.item .polaroid:before {
  content: ";
  position: absolute;
  z-index: -1;
  transition: all 0.35s;
}

.item:nth-of-type(4n+1) {
  transform: scale(0.8, 0.8) rotate(5deg);
}

.item:nth-of-type(4n+1) .polaroid:before {
  @extend %imgeffect;
  transform: rotate(6deg);
}

.item:nth-of-type(4n+2) {
  transform: scale(0.8, 0.8) rotate(-5deg);
}

.item:nth-of-type(4n+2) .polaroid:before {
  @extend %imgeffect;
  transform: rotate(-6deg);
}

.item:nth-of-type(4n+3) {
  transform: scale(0.8, 0.8) rotate(-3deg);
}

.item:nth-of-type(4n+3) .polaroid:before {
  @extend %imgeffect;
  transform: rotate(-4deg);
}
```

5. This final set of rules applies a rotation and scaling effect when we hover over each image; we also tweak the size and box-shadow effect at the same time:

```
.item:hover {
  filter: none;
  transform: scale(1, 1) rotate(0deg);
  transition: all 0.35s;
}
```

```
.item:hover .polaroid:before {
  z-index: -1;
  transform: rotate(0deg);
  height: 90%;
  width: 90%;
  bottom: 0%;
  right: 5%;
  box-shadow: 0 16px 48px rgba(0,0,0,0.2);
  transition: all 0.35s;
}
```

6. Save the file as `extend.scss` in the `scss` folder.

7. Next, fire up a terminal session and change the working folder to the `extend` folder under our project area.

8. At the prompt, type the following command and press Enter:

```
sass sass\extend.scss css\extend.css
```

9. If all is well, we should see a `extend.css` file appear in the `css` folder, along with a source map – previewing the results will show our three images styled as Polaroids, with the center one in mid-hover (Figure 3-6).

Introducing Sass: Applying a Polaroid effect

Figure 3-6. *Displaying images using @extend*

This demo is something of trip down memory lane – this CSS styling effect has been around for a few years. However, there is a little bit of a sting in this tale though: before we discover what it is, let's take a look at how our code works in more detail.

Dissecting Our Code in Detail

Our Polaroid-inspired demo contains what at first glance looks like a good chunk of styling code, but in reality, much of this is used to style each image. There are two key declarations that we should explore, though, which use Sass and help make our demo come to life. They are the extend block:

```
%imgeffect {
  height: 20%;
  width: 47%;
  bottom: 30px;
  right: 12px;
  box-shadow: 0 33.6px 32px rgba(0,0,0,0.4);
}
```

... and the three declarations where we make use of this extend:

```
.item:nth-of-type(4n+1) .polaroid:before {
  @extend %imgeffect;
  transform: rotate(6deg);
}

.item:nth-of-type(4n+2) .polaroid:before {
  @extend %imgeffect;
  transform: rotate(-6deg);
}

.item:nth-of-type(4n+3) .polaroid:before {
  @extend %imgeffect;
  transform: rotate(-4deg);
}
```

If we were to compile this into valid CSS, we would end up with the code shown in Figure 3-7.

```
CSS
1▾ .item:nth-of-type(4n+2) .polaroid:before, .item:nth-of-type(4n+1) .polaroid:before {
2     height: 20%;
3     width: 47%;
4     bottom: 30px;
5     right: 12px;
6     box-shadow: 0 33.6px 32px rgba(0, 0, 0, 0.4);
7  }
8
9▾ .item:nth-of-type(4n+1) .polaroid:before {
10    transform: rotate(6deg);
11 }
12
13▾ .item:nth-of-type(4n+2) .polaroid:before {
14    transform: rotate(-6deg);
15 }
```

Figure 3-7. *Compiling code from our @extend demo*

In our demo, we've specified our initial extend in lines 1 to 7; this contains a standard set of CSS properties, which are used in each Polaroid effect. The extend is called as part of defining the three `.item:nth-of-type()` declarations, one for each instance of the Polaroid effect. Figure 3-7 shows a screenshot of two instances of our `item:nth-of-type()` declarations compiled in Sassmeister as an example of how it will look, where we can indeed see the common class displayed before the additional variations.

Try it for yourself using the online tool at Sassmeister.com – I've not included the third instance as only two is enough to show the effect of using the extend function.

Some of you may have spotted something from earlier in this chapter, where we talked about both the base class *and the extended class* being present. I don't see the base class present, although in theory it should be displayed – why isn't it?

Using Extends or Mixins?

Aha – there is a good reason for this: we're deliberately stopping Sass from displaying it. However, there is more to it than just hiding code – it has much to do with how extends work, similarities with mixins, and why it is important to choose the right function when writing code.

Although both mixins and extends are very similar, there are two key differences we should be aware of:

- The extend rule doesn't take parameters – mixins do.

- The extend rule can combine selectors, whereas mixins don't.

Put simply, extends are more efficient than mixins, but they don't give us any opportunity to be flexible about values that we might otherwise pass to mixins. The best way to illustrate this is with an example; here's the Sass part of the code from the previous demo, rewritten using a mixin:

```
@mixin imgeffect {
  height: 20%;
  width: 47%;
  bottom: 30px;
  right: 12px;
  box-shadow: 0 33.6px 32px rgba(0,0,0,0.4);
}

.item:nth-of-type(4n+1) .polaroid:before {
  @include imgeffect;
  transform: rotate(6deg);
}

.item:nth-of-type(4n+2) .polaroid:before {
  @include imgeffect;
  transform: rotate(-6deg);
}

.item:nth-of-type(4n+3) .polaroid:before {
  @include imgeffect;
  transform: rotate(-4deg);
}
```

Try dropping this into a Sassmeister session – notice how, although it compiles correctly (producing 26 lines of code), it contains a great deal of repetition?

Clearly this isn't ideal – it will work, but compiling code in this manner will soon add a lot of extra bloat to our style sheet, and slow our site down. It's for this reason that we need to be careful about whether we use a mixin or extend – there are some other considerations we should take into account when choosing what to use:

- As extends can't accept parameters, this makes them less flexible than mixins – they are best suited to replicating the same styles across multiple elements, and where different properties are set by exception.

- We can't use extends when creating responsive media directives; only mixins can be used in this instance.

- When using classes that contain extended code, any subclasses we then specify will automatically contain the extended code too. This can make for some odd effects if we're not careful!

- On a more technical note – many people will claim that extends are faster than mixins. However, with modern server technologies (such as file compression), this isn't always the case; in fact, mixins can be more effective, as strings are frequently repeated, which works better for compression.

So – thinking back to our code: we can use either an extend or mixin in our instance. I chose to use an extend rule to illustrate how they work, but if you have server-based compression enabled (as do many servers), then you might decide to use a mixin instead. Ultimately it is all about taking care; it will depend on how your code is set up, and the number of levels your styles are set, as to which route you take when using mixins or extends.

Summary

The art of nesting and inheriting styles in Sass is a key topic – it's one where the basics might be easy to learn, but mastering it can be a real skill! Over the course of this chapter, we've been introduced to both nesting and use of the extend rule, so let's take a moment to review what we have learned.

We kicked off this chapter by exploring how to nest our code – we understood that it helped to avoid repetition and reduce the amount of code we have to write. This was swiftly followed by a look at some of the pitfalls we might encounter when nesting code; at the same time, we discussed whether nesting is a bad practice, or just one that requires a certain amount of care when used.

Moving on, we then switched to covering the use of parent selectors; we examined how this is essential for instances such as nesting pseudo-elements in code. We then took an in-depth look at the basics around the @extend directive – this included working through a detailed example before weighing up the pros and cons of using extends or mixins, given the similarities between both in Sass.

Okay – let's move on: we often have to write code that determines the outcome only after satisfying a condition. It's an all-too common technique when writing script, but what about if we were creating styles? Plain CSS doesn't allow for this, so styles have to be written statically. Not anymore: it's time to turn the tables and start to use scripting techniques to control our CSS styles too …

CHAPTER 4

Calculating Values Using Operations

One of the key benefits to using Sass is the ability to calculate values dynamically – I don't just mean by using something like percentage values, but working out values using operators such as addition or subtraction.

Yes, you read correctly – using math! Now, before you run for the hills, this isn't as crazy as it may seem: we can already write statements such as `font: 10px/8px;` in our code. As Sass is an extension of CSS, Sass not only supports this, but takes it to a whole new level. The great thing about this though is that the math involved does not have to be complicated at all – it can be as simple as adding two numbers together, or dividing a number.

With this in mind, let's take a look at the different type of operations we can perform using Sass, starting with some number-based operations.

Number-Based Operations

All of the standard operations such as addition or division are supported (including relational operators such as >=); it means we can write a declaration such as this:

```
p {
  $width: 780px;
  width: $width/2;
}
```

© Alex Libby 2019
A. Libby, *Introducing Dart Sass*, https://doi.org/10.1007/978-1-4842-4372-5_4

... which will compile to:

```
p { width: 390px; }
```

Operators for String-Based Content

There are two main uses for operators when working with strings: we can concatenate text together or perform inline calculations using string interpolation. The latter isn't complicated – it requires us to place our calculation inside curly brackets and precede this with a #, which tells Sass to calculate the total, as shown in this example:

```
p:before {
  content: "I ate #{5 + 10} large " + apples;
}
```

Boolean-Based Operators

On occasion, it may be useful to include declarations based on a condition being true or false; the declaration will be included if true, otherwise it will be omitted. Our third operation type allows Boolean values to control what is displayed:

```
p:before {
  $count: 5;
  $yes: 1;
  @if ($count > 3 and $yes == 1) {
    content: "I ate #{5 + 10} large " + apples;
  }
}
```

When compiled, we get the following result:

```
p:before {
  content: "I ate 15 large apples";
}
```

List-Based Operators

The final category covers all of the types of operations we can perform on lists of data used in Sass. Lists are a useful way to group together similar properties we might use later in our code, such as colors or border types, so that we can control what is used in our code:

```
$colors: red green blue;
$padding: 10px, 20px, 30px;
$border: solid, dotted;
```

With the list defined, we can use a function such as nth to choose an item from that list, in this case green:

```
div {
  background: nth($colours, 2);
  padding: nth($padding, 2); // "20px"
  border: 2px nth($border, 2));
}
```

This results in the following code, when compiled:

```
div {
  background: green;
  padding: 20px;
  border: 2px dotted;
}
```

List items can be delineated using commas or spaces, but if you are using the latter, then properties should be encased in quotes, and the unquote() function should be used to remove them in code.

We've only touched the surface of the different types of operations that are p[possible using Sass – the main website documents all of the functions available, at `http://sass-lang.com/documentation/Sass/Script/Functions.html`.

Okay – let's move on: the examples we've used are somewhat theoretical; to really see how they work, we should create something that shows off how they work. A great example is by creating a grid-based page template, so without further ado, let's dive in and see how this works in practice.

Putting This Into Practice

For our next demo, we're going to make use of Sass's operations to create a basic skeleton page, where values for widths such as the main content block are worked out automatically for us. We'll make use of one additional resource in this demo, in the form of a script font – Homemade Apple, which is available for download from `https://www.fontsquirrel.com/fonts/homemade-apple` in WOFF format (which should cover most recent browsers).

CREATING A FRAMEWORK

Let's make a start on building our demo:

1. We'll begin by extracting a copy of the `skeleton` folder from the code download that accompanies this book – go ahead and save it to the root of our project folder.

2. Our demo contains all of the relevant markup already in place,
    but if we were to run it now, it will look awful! It's at this point
    we need to add styling – for this, we have a fair few rules to
    add, so let's make a start with some basic styles for fonts and
    links used in the site:

```
@font-face { font-family: 'pt_sansregular'; src: url('../
font/pt_sansregular.woff') format('woff'); font-weight:
normal; font-style: normal; }

@font-face { font-family: 'homemade_appleregular'; src:
url('../font/HomemadeApple-webfont.woff') format('woff');
font-weight: normal; font-style: normal; }

body { font-family: 'pt_sansregular', sans-serif; margin:
32px;
  width: 900px; }

a {
  text-decoration: none;
  &:hover {
    color: #6db046;
  }
}

#container {
  width: 100%;
  border: 1px solid black;
  min-height: 100px;
  background-color: #f5f5f5;
  > p > i {
    padding-right: 3px;
  }
}
```

3. Next up comes the key to this demo – we're adding the styles
    for the main part of the page, header, footer, and sidebar:

```css
article[role="main"], header {
  float: left;
  width: 600px / 960px * 100%;
  margin: 15px 0px 15px 15px;
  padding: 10px;
}

article[role="main"] {
  min-height: 500px;
  background-color: #fff;
  padding: 15px;
}

header {
  height: 55px; padding: 10px 10px 0 0px; margin: 15px 0 0 15px;

  h2{
    font-family: 'homemade_appleregular'; font-size: 30px;
    margin-top: 5px; color: #6db046;
  }
}

aside {
  float: right;
  width: 200px / 960px * 100%;
  margin: 100px 15px 15px 10px;
  float: left;
  padding: 10px;
  min-height: 200px;
  background-color: #fff;
  ul {
    padding-left: 25px;
```

```
     h3 {
       border-bottom: 1px solid green;
       margin-left: -20px;
     }
   }
 }

footer { clear: both; background-color: #6db046;
padding: 10px; width: 880px; }
```

4. We now need to add in styling for some of the detail – the next three rules cover the images shown at the foot of the page, the comments tag, and date of posting, respectively:

```
section { margin-left: auto; margin-right: auto;
width: 600px; }

.details { font-size: 14px; clear: both; padding-top: 5px;
  border-top: 1px solid #6db046; }

.date {
  width: 250px / 960px * 100%;
  font-size: 14px;
  clear: both;
  padding-top: 5px;
  margin-left: 15px;
  border-top: 1px solid #000;
}
```

5. Within the <section> block at the foot of our page, we've added in images – these need adjusting, using the following styles:

```
.subimage { width: 275px / 960px * 100%; border: 1px
solid brown; height: 175px; clear: both; display: inline-
block;   margin-right: 15px; }
img { width: 100%; height: auto; }
```

6. Last, but by no means least, we'll add in the final rule to take care of styling the labeling for each of the images:

```
.tileText { width: 100%; height: 30px; padding: 0px 5px
0px 5px; display: block; font-weight: bold; }
```

7. Save the file as `skeleton.scss` in the `scss` folder.

8. Next, fire up a terminal session and change the working folder to the `skeleton` folder under our project area.

9. At the prompt, type the following command and press Enter:

```
sass sass\skeleton.scss css\skeleton.css
```

10. If all is well, we should see a `skeleton.css` file appear in the `css` folder, along with a source map – previewing the results will show a simple template page with styled elements, as indicated in Figure 4-1.

Introducing Dart SASS: Creating a Skeleton Site

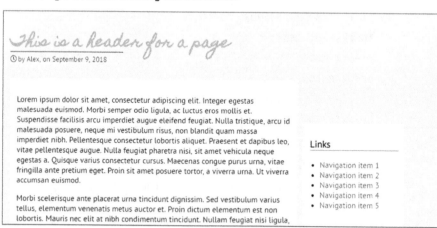

Figure 4-1. *Creating a skeleton page template*

Our demo shows how easy it is to create templates when using Sass – indeed, the basic principles we've used here can easily form the basis of many of the grid systems available for use today. However, there are a couple of key points to note; before we cover them, let's take a look at the code we've created in more detail.

Understanding What Happened

Although the code we've used looks lengthy, in reality much of it is used to style existing elements such as font sizes or colors. We have, however, used standard Sass nesting to lay out each rule within our style sheet – Sass will recompile each into valid CSS during compilation.

The key parts of interest to us though, lie on or around lines 40, 65, 101, and 110, where we have code similar to this:

```
width: 200px / 960px * 100%;
```

Sass automatically calculates this equation during compilation; if we were to take the rule we created for article[role="main"] and header (which specifies width: 600px / 960px * 100%), and pasted it into Sassmeister, it would give us this compiled code (Figure 4-2).

```
CSS
1 ▾ article[role=main], header {
2      float: left;
3      width: 62.5%;
4      margin: 15px 0px 15px 15px;
5      padding: 10px;
6   }
```

Figure 4-2. Viewing the results of a calculation

Although it's not 100% obvious, the calculation used is based on the principle of the Golden Ratio. This ratio has helped quantify what makes certain designs more pleasing than others – it's all about ensuring that proportions of larger elements are twice that of smaller ones. In our case though, the numbers are not quite there – `62.5%` of 960px (our base measurement) equates to 600px, whereas if we follow the ratio exactly, it should be nearer 594px. Hey – what's 6px in a demo design?

If you would like to learn more about this principle, then Google has plenty of references to articles online, such as `https://www.interaction-design.org/literature/article/the-golden-ratio-principles-of-form-and-layout`.

Performing simple math in Sass is just the tip of the iceberg, with regard to what is possible: there is a host of other functions we can use! They range from manipulating strings, to numbers, and even changing colors – we can work out the lengths of strings, cut them into smaller chunks, or even create a palette of new colors from existing values. This is one area that is well worth becoming familiar with, so let's dive in and take a look at some examples in more detail.

Defining Functions

If you spend any time writing styles for websites, then I am sure you'll appreciate the need to specify absolute values for properties, such as `background-color()` or `font-size()`. It's a real drag, but what if I said you may not have to ...?

Yes – that's right: once you start using Sass, there will be occasions where you don't have to work out values manually: you can get Sass to do the heavy lifting for you. Sass borrows many of its function principles from scripting languages such as JavaScript – indeed, many will say that this is one area where the lines between JavaScript and CSS really begins to blur!

That aside, functions within Sass can be split into several categories, which are summarized in Table 4-1.

Table 4-1. *Function Types Available in Sass*

Group	Description (with examples)
Colors (including opacity)	This splits into three categories – RGB, HSL, and opacity; this grouping covers functions such as saturation() or hsl(), which are designed to get or manipulate colors.
Strings	This group of functions allows us to manipulate strings using Sass – performing tasks such as changing text case, inserting characters into strings, and getting the length of a string.
Numbers	We've already seen how you can use basic operators in Sass, such as addition – this group takes it up a level with functions such as round(), abs(), and random().
Lists	This group of functions allows us to manipulate Sass lists, such operations such as length() or nth() to get a specific item from a list. **Note:** lists are immutable in Sass, so will return a new list, rather than update an existing one in place.
Maps	Maps are a relatively new feature in Sass – they allow us to create a configuration area, rather than have to create multiple single variables. This group of functions allows us to get and manipulate content within maps, using functions such as map-get() or map-values().

(continued)

Table 4-1. (*continued*)

Group	Description (with examples)
Selectors	If we need to perform tasks such as joining selectors, or replacing one with another within our Sass code – this group of functions allows us to do this, using commands such as `selector-append()` or `selector-unify()`.
Introspection	This group of functions helps determine if certain functions, variables, or mixins exist in the current scope within our code, or can return the type associated with a value.
Miscellaneous	This contains two functions that don't sit within any of the other groups – `if()` and `unique-id()`. Note: the `if()` function is a *ternary operator* in this context, and not a conditional function as we will see later in this chapter.

The full list of functions is available on the main Sass website at `http://sass-lang.com/documentation/Sass/Script/Functions.html`.

To fully understand how these functions work, would be outside of the scope of this book – indeed, we could probably write a tome just on the subject in its own right!

This said, it's worth spending time on exploring at least part of what is available within the world of Sass functions. Over the course of the next few pages, we're going to dive into manipulating Sass colors as a mini case study; it goes without saying that color is so important, and this is one area where Sass can really help with producing code in our development process.

Working with Colors – a Mini Case Study

A site without color would be like life without excitement – very boring! Indeed, not only does color add that extra sparkle to a site, it can also help convey a message: for example, red in China conveys a sense of happiness.

In the past, we might have specified an array of colors in our palette – not only is this time consuming to get right, it is also a real pain to keep updated, particularly if clients change their mind at the last minute!

To help with this, Sass contains a host of different functions that allow us to manipulate colors in a manner of different ways. For example, we can adjust the saturation levels, change the brightness, or alter the hue of a color – the list is endless. To see how this might look in action, take a look at `http://jackiebalzer.com/color`: this only specifies two colors but contains over 30 different shades, created using Sass functions. This is just one example: a quick look online shows other similar examples, such as these:

- `http://scg.ar-ch.org/` – enter a color to get the hex codes for various shades, such as lighten or desaturate;

- `http://jim-nielsen.com/sassme/` – use the sliders to generate a new color, and grab the code for use in a style sheet;

- `https://codepen.io/KatieK2/pen/hbqsB` – more experiments using color functions;

- `https://css-tricks.com/snippets/sass/tint-shade-functions/` – two custom functions created by Hugo Giraudel, to get a slightly lighter or darker shade of a color.

Let's put one of these functions to use, and adjust the color used to fill in an SVG image – the base color is a shade of light gray; we'll make it even lighter using the `lighten()` function.

MANIPULATING COLORS

Let's make a start on creating our demo:

1. We'll start by downloading a copy of the `colorfunctions` folder from the code download that accompanies this book – go ahead and save it to our project folder.

2. Next, open a new document and add the following rules:

   ```
   @font-face { font-family: 'pt_sansregular'; src: url('../
   font/pt_sansregular.woff') format('woff'); font-weight:
   normal; font-style: normal; }
   ```

   ```
   body { font-family: 'pt_sansregular', sans-serif; margin:
   32px; width: 850px; }
   ```

   ```
   ellipse { fill: lighten(#c6c6c6, 8); }
   ```

3. Save the file as `colorfunctions.scss` in the `scss` folder.

4. Next, fire up a terminal session and change the working folder to the `colorfunctions` folder under our project area.

5. At the prompt, type the following command and press Enter:

   ```
   sass sass\colorfunctions.scss css\colorfunctions.css
   ```

6. If all is well, we should see a `colorfunctions.css` file appear in the `css` folder, along with a source map – previewing the results will show a simple template page with styled elements, as indicated in Figure 4-3.

Introducing SASS: Changing Color with Color Functions

Figure 4-3. *Adjusting a color within an SVG image*

This is a very basic demo, but it is designed to show how easy it is to use a Sass color function. In this instance, we used `fill:` as this is required when using SVG images; we could easily have used background-color or color if it was for a standard HTML element. Our demo increased the lightness of the initial value by a factor of 8%, from #c6c6c6 to #dadada – we could easily specify this as a new color for another element, rather than create a new variable that will use valuable resources.

Let's step things up a few notches and create something a little more practical – how about creating a color palette for a website? Yes, you heard me correctly – this is a perfect opportunity for Sass to do the heavy lifting for us; we only need to specify one color and let Sass create every other color for us automatically.

The great thing though is that we don't even have to work out the math involved to generate our target color – we can use a tool hosted at http:// razorltd.github.io/sasscolourfunctioncalculator/ to provide the transformation for us. To see how this works, we're going to make use of an example palette from the Color Palettes website at http://colorpalettes. net/ and get Sass to generate the colors for us during compilation.

PART 2 – CREATING COLORS

Let's begin creating our demo:

1. We'll start by downloading and extracting a copy of the palette folder from the code download that accompanies this book – go ahead and save it to our project folder.

2. We need to add our styles; so for this, go ahead and open a new document. There are a good few present, so we'll add them block by block, starting with some base styles:

   ```
   $basecolor: #213451;

   @font-face { font-family: 'pt_sansregular'; src: url('../
   font/pt_sansregular.woff') format('woff'); font-weight:
   normal; font-style: normal; }

   body { font-family: 'pt_sansregular', sans-serif;
   margin: 32px; width: 850px; }

   #palette { margin-bottom: 15px; }
   ```

3. With the base styles in place, we can now add the rules to style each swatch:

   ```
   .swatch { height: 125px; width: 75px; display: inline-
   block;    margin-right: 17px; }

   .swlabel { border: 1px solid #bfbfbf; width: 75px;
   display: inline-block; margin-right: 15px; margin-top:
   -15px; text-align: center; padding: 10px 0px 10px 0;}
   ```

4. To give each swatch color, we need to add in the following rules to our style sheet:

   ```
   .swatch:nth-child(1) { background-color: $basecolor; }

   .swatch:nth-child(2) {
   ```

```scss
  background-color: lighten(desaturate($basecolor,
  22.27), 30.20);
}

.swatch:nth-child(3) {
  background-color: lighten(desaturate(adjust-
  hue($basecolor, 119), 15.54), 52.55);
}

.swatch:nth-child(4) {
  background-color: lighten(desaturate(adjust-
  hue($basecolor, 114), 32.11), 73.73);
}

.swatch:nth-child(5) {
  background-color: lighten(saturate(adjust-hue(#213451,
  -131), 57.89), 4.90);
}
```

5. Save the file as palette.scss in the scss folder.

6. Next, fire up a terminal session and change the working folder to the palette folder under our project area.

7. At the prompt, type the following command and press Enter:

```
sass sass\palette.scss css\palette.css
```

8. If all is well, we should see a palette.css file appear in the css folder, along with a source map – previewing the results will show a simple template page with styled elements, as indicated in Figure 4-4.

Introducing Dart Sass: Creating Colors with Functions

| #213451 | #6e819e | #d0aebc | #f6f4f5 | #508b00 |

Figure 4-4. *Creating a color palette with Sass*

Although the Sass code in this demo may look complex, in reality we don't have to worry about the specifics, as most of the heavy lifting is done for via the Sass color function tool we used in this demo. There are nevertheless some really useful benefits to creating palettes in this manner, so let's dive in and take a look at our code in more detail.

Breaking Apart the Code in Detail

The traditional approach to creating palettes would likely take the form of choosing colors, then deciding which should be used and where, and hoping that we retain some form of consistency during development! (I'm sure this sounds worse than it really is, but nevertheless it is a manual approach that is opens us to a degree of risk.)

When you first start with Sass, though, the temptation might be to assign different colors to variables – so you might have $white for white, and $desaturatedblue would represent #213451. Creating variables though is tedious – we have to make sure all of the colors complement each other, and that our general palette looks sensible (and fits in with brand guidelines).

Instead, we can flip things entirely on its head – while a good chunk of code sets up each swatch, we only specify one base color, at line 16. Although this may seem crazy, there is a good reason for this – we transform the base color to become each of the palette colors chosen for this demo. If we take a look at the middle one, which has this set as its color:

```
background-color: lighten(desaturate(adjust-hue($basecolor, 119),
15.54), 52.55);
```

... we can break it down into its constituent parts:

- `adjust-hue($basecolor, 119)` – this gives us our first intermediate color (or color1);

- `desaturate(color1, 15.54)` – this results in our second color (or color2);

- `lighten(color2, 52.55)` – our third and final color.

In this instance, we've created 3 new colors that could be used in their own right; instead, we're getting Sass to automatically calculate color3 directly from our base color in a single pass. The same principles apply to each of the colors we've created for the palette – our calculations have resulted in a total of 11 colors that could be created from just 1 color!

To see the effect of splitting this calculation, take a look at `https://gist.github.com/alexlibby/6fd1492781a08757c0112bb85c7a832a`. This shows the big calculation split into rheww separate entries. Notice how `p:nth-child(3)` equals `p:nth-child(4)` – our code steps through each calculation, using the results from the previous color change as the basis for the new one.

Assessing the Benefits from Using this Approach

It might seem a complex way to create colors, but there are some good reasons for using this approach:

- We can always perform a search and replace, but what happens if our code uses a slightly different spelling of a color or variable? The search and replace may not pick it up, leading to unexpected effects in our code.

- If a client asks for a last-minute change, then you only have one value that needs updating; everything else is worked out automatically during compilation.

- We don't need to create variables for each color – although compiling a calculation such as ours may take a few seconds more, we are not compiling code "on-the-fly," so we can live with the extra compiling time required.

Of course, if we end up with a monster style sheet (and I'm talking tens of thousands of lines), then this extra compilation time may start to add up – if this is the case, we may prefer to use variables instead.

Okay – let's crack on: we've touched on some of the functions available and explored how we might use them in a practical context in our code. Although this introduces an element of dynamism to our code, we're still limited in as much as our functions will result in one value (as was the case in the last demo).

What happens if we need to specify different values, based on satisfying set conditions? Well, Sass can help here – it borrows techniques from scripting language such as JavaScript to implement features such as loops. It's an important part of the library that is well worth exploring, so let's take a look at the features available that we can use to evaluate conditions in our Sass code, in more detail.

Evaluating Conditions

Decisions, decisions – do we use this color, or another ...? What about positioning that content at the top of the page ...?

Our lives are full of decisions that have to be made – in most cases, we will make the right one, but sometimes we may not! The same applies to styling content: we might choose a color that ends up clashing with others used on the site, or a background color we apply ends up making text illegible.

One of the key benefits of using Sass, though, is that we can build in a certain amount of control to reduce these issues – if the color of an element is particularly dark, then Sass can be told to select a lighter color so our content remains legible.

How can we achieve this? Well, it's time we met Sass's Control Directives and Expressions! This mouthful of a name represents a group of functions that allow us to control which styles are used and when – it's worth noting that they are intended more for use in mixins, but can be used in day-to-day styling if required. Let's take a look at each of them, beginning with the @if functions.

Applying @if and @if():

Let's say for argument's sake we had run into an issue of clashing colors, caused as a result of insufficient contrast – how would we solve this problem? Well, one way to solve it would, of course, be to replace the offending color, but this is a manual task that requires effort. Instead, how about getting Sass to choose for us?

No problem – Sass has two functions that can help here: ironically both are called @if, but they each have different uses! The first, @if(), takes this format: if(true, 1px, 2px) => 1px – it is used to decide if we should apply the first value (1px), or choose 2px if that variable doesn't exist or might cause an error (such as divide by zero).

The second is more straightforward – we can use @if to decide if we include a value or not, such as in this example: @if 1 + 1 == 2 { border: 1px solid; }, which will render as true. If it had rendered as false, then the border property simply wouldn't be set. Both can be a little tricky to fully understand, so let's create a demo to explore how these two work in more detail.

USING IF STATEMENTS

The first step is to grab a copy of the download that accompanies this book – once you have it, follow these steps:

1. We'll start by downloading and extracting a copy of the example condition folder from the code download that accompanies this book – go ahead and save it to our project folder.

2. Our demo doesn't contain the Sass styles needed to make it work – for this, go ahead and create a new file, saving it as condition.scss in the sass subfolder in the condition folder we saved in step 1.

3. We have a few style rules to add in, which we will add in block by block, starting with some basic styles required to set up our demo:

```
@font-face { font-family: 'pt_sansregular'; src: url('../
font/pt_sansregular.woff') format('woff'); font-weight:
normal; font-style: normal; }

body { font-family: 'pt_sansregular', sans-serif;
margin: 32px; font-size: 20px; }

li { padding: 20px 5px; margin: 10px; color: white;
width: 400px; list-style: none; }
```

4. Next up comes the crux of our demo – we first specify three colors, which are defined by the outcomes of three if statements:

```
$first-color: if(true, antiquewhite, black);
$second-color: if(false, black, slategrey);
$third-color: if(4 > 2, silver, black);
```

5. We now need to add in the conditions that determine some of the properties used in each of the four list items:

```
li:nth-of-type(1) {
  background: $first-color;
  @if (lightness($first-color) > 75%) {
      color: black;
    } @else {
      color: white;
    }
}

li:nth-of-type(2) {
  @if 1 + 1 == 2 { background: $second-color;  }
  @if 5 > 3 { border: 3px dotted $third-color;
  width: 394px; }
  @if true { font-family: 'sans-serif'; }
}

li:nth-of-type(3) {
  background: $third-color;
  @if (lightness($third-color) > 75%) {
      color: black;
    } @else {
      color: white;
    }
}
```

```
li:nth-of-type(4) {
  @if 1 + 1 == 2 { background: darken($second-color, 50%); }
  @else if 1 + 2 == 3 { background: $second-color; }
  @else if 5 > 3{ border: 2px dotted $third-color; }
}
```

6. Go ahead and save the file – next, fire up a terminal session and change the working folder to the condition folder under our project area.

7. At the prompt, type the following command and press Enter:

    ```
    sass sass\condition.scss css\condition.css
    ```

8. If all is well, we should see a colorfunctions.css file appear in the css folder, along with a source map – previewing the results will show a simple template page with styled elements, as indicated in Figure 4-5.

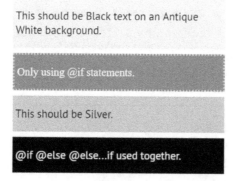

Introducing Dart Sass: Using @If or @Else

Figure 4-5. *Using @if...@else statements*

At first glance our demo looks very simple, with straightforward styling for each list item. However, under the covers it hides a fair amount of decision making that determines which color each list item should use! We've used two key functions within this demo that are important to understand, so let's take a few minutes to explore how they work in more detail.

Understanding What Happened

The first part of the style sheet for our demo contains some standard rules that we use to define some basic styling for the demo and each list item. The crux of our demo though starts on line 22, where we use three @if() statements to create our colors.

The simplest way to understand how these work, is to say, "If condition is X, we use the first value (true), otherwise we use the second (false)." For the first one, we specify antique white as the truthy color; as our condition is set to true, this is the color that will be used in our style sheet.

For the second type of @if statement, where we're setting three properties for the second list item, we simply need to satisfy each condition. If the answer is correct (i.e., true), then the attribute shown in brackets is applied; if not, it is discarded.

The remaining two examples work in the same way as the first two – list item three uses the same principle as the first list item, with the fourth following the same technique as the second list item.

113

Looping Through Styles

One of Sass's key abilities is taking over the effort of generating styles – for example, we can use functions to create an entire color palette, or get Sass to choose what color to apply to a background, so that it doesn't clash with foreground colors.

This is just a small part though of what Sass can achieve – where Sass really comes into its own is iterating through multiple elements, applying styles to each from a single set of instructions. For example, how about creating a set of payment card icons for an e-commerce site – we can create a common set of styles, but use Sass to create those styles unique to each image, from a single list of names.

Sass has a number of functions that are suited to this kind of task – they each have their own unique traits, but each work on a similar principle of iterating through a group of items. Let's take a look at each in turn, beginning with the @for function.

Working with @for

The first of our functions, @for, is used to repeatedly create a set of styles – it uses a counter to iterate through each instance of that style, adjusting each based on what is specified in the directive. The syntax for this directive is very straightforward: @for $var from <start> through <end>, with the changes enclosed in brackets.

There is a second format you can use – replace the word through with to, which works equally well.

Let's take a look at how this function works in detail, with a quick demo.

APPLYING STYLES USING @FOR

Let's make a start on setting up our demo:

1. We'll begin by downloading and extracting a copy of the forloop folder from the code download that comes with this book; go ahead and save it to our project folder.

2. The download contains all of the markup, but this will be useless without our styling, so let's create a new file, saving it as forloop.scss in the sass folder for this demo.

3. In the file, go ahead and add the following code blocks in turn, beginning with some basic styles to set up our demo:

```
$basecolor: #213451;

@font-face {
  font-family: 'pt_sansregular';
  src: url('../font/pt_sansregular.woff') format('woff');
  font-weight: normal;
  font-style: normal;
}

body { font-family: 'pt_sansregular', sans-serif; margin:
32px;}

ul { width: 150px; background-color: rgba(0,0,0,0.6) }
```

4. The remaining rules form the crux of our demo – these take care of styling each list item:

```
$rainbow: silver slategrey antiquewhite darkgrey
gainsboro;
@for $i from 1 through 5 {
  li:nth-child(#{$i}) {
    color: nth($rainbow, $i);
```

115

```
      font-size: 32px;
      font-weight: bold;
    }
  }
```

5. Go ahead and save the file – next, fire up a terminal session and change the working folder to the `forloop` folder under our project area.

6. At the prompt, type the following command and press Enter:

```
sass sass\forloop.scss css\forloop.css
```

7. If all is well, we should see a `forloop.css` file appear in the `css` folder, along with a source map – previewing the results will show a simple template page with styled elements, as indicated in Figure 4-6.

Introducing Dart Sass: Looping through Styles

Figure 4-6. *Looping through styles with @for*

Hehe – I bet you didn't know a demo could be so friendly! Okay – yes, that was a terrible joke, but leaving aside the content, our demo shows of a useful concept that is worth coming to grips with when developing using Sass. Let's take a look at that concept in more detail.

Understanding How Our Code Works

So – what is that concept that we speak of? It's one of repetition – we have five items that form a simple list: all of which need styling, but not all with the same values!

Our demo consists of five list items in a simple unordered list – as most of the styles are similar, we only need write one instance of it and use a Sass for loop to iterate through each item, in turn, to apply the appropriate styles:

```
$rainbow: silver slategrey antiquewhite darkgrey gainsboro;
@for $i from 1 through 5 {
  li:nth-child(#{$i}) {
    color: nth($rainbow, $i);
    font-size: 32px;
    font-weight: bold;
  }
}
```

The catch though is the color attribute – as we want to apply different colors, we create a list, and assign this to the variable $rainbow. In our for loop, we then count through this list and apply a color to each in turn, which is formatted using string interpolation (replacing (#{$i}) with the appropriate number). When compiled, the code for each of the list items will look something like the example shown in Figure 4-7.

```
li:nth-child(1) {
  color:  silver;
  font-size: 32px;
  font-weight: bold;
}
```

Figure 4-7. *Styling a list item*

This is a great way to apply styles, but the key thing to remember is that of repetition – the items we are targeting must be of the same type. In this instance, we were targeting list items; elements of other types would have to be styled separately.

Looping Using @each

This next looping function is a little more complex – it is not a loop function as such, but we are looping through multiple items! Let me explain what I mean:

The @each function allows us to set a variable to each item in a list or Sass map – a list is just a comma-separated set of values. A map takes this up a level – it allows us to assign multiple values to a single item, where they relate to the same item. For example, we might be talking about a group of cars – the properties could be color, make, model: these each apply to each car.

We will revisit the subject of Sass maps in more detail, later in this chapter.

To see what this means in practice, we're going to create a simple demo that sets up a number of buttons using the @each function – for each, we're going to specify the color and button function using a Sass list, then iterate through each to create our final style rules.

```
STYLING EACH ITEM
```

Let's make a start on our demo:

1. We'll begin by downloading a copy of the eachitem folder from the code download that accompanies this book – save it to the root of our project folder.

2. Next, we need to add in our Sass styling – for this, go ahead and create a new file, saving it as eachitem.scss in the sass subfolder in the condition folder we saved in step 1.

3. We have a few style rules to add in, which we will add in block by block, starting with some basic styles required to set up our demo:

```
@import url(https://fonts.googleapis.com/
css?family=Poiret+One);

@font-face {
  font-family: 'pt_sansregular';
  src: url('../font/pt_sansregular.woff') format('woff');
  font-weight: normal;
  font-style: normal;
}

body {
  font-family: 'pt_sansregular', sans-serif;
  margin: 32px;
}
```

4. Next up are some initial values we create, along with a Sass list to store values in pairs (each pair containing the button type and a variable pointing to its color):

```
$publish: gainsboro;
$postpone: antiquewhite;
$delete: silver;

$states: (publish, $publish),
         (postpone, $postpone),
         (delete, $delete);
```

5. With our base values in place, we can now style our button –
   for this, go ahead and add the following code:

```scss
@each $buttonstate, $color in $states {

    button { color: #000; text-decoration: none; padding:
    5px 10px; border-radius: 3px; font-family: 'Poiret One',
    cursive; font-size: 32px; font-weight: bold; outline: 0; }

    .#{$buttonstate} {
      padding: 10px 20px;
      border: none;
      background-color: $color;

      &:hover { background-color: darken( $color, 10% );
            transition: all 0.3s ease; }
      &:active { background: darken($color,25%); }
    }
}
```

6. Go ahead and save the file – next, fire up a terminal session
   and change the working folder to the easchitem folder under
   our project area.

7. At the prompt, type the following command and press Enter:

```
sass sass\eachitem.scss css\eachitem.css
```

8. If all is well, we should see a colorfunctions.css file
   appear in the css folder, along with a source map – previewing
   the results will show a simple template page with styled
   elements, as indicated in Figure 4-8.

Introducing Dart Sass: Using @Each

Figure 4-8. *Creating button styles using @each*

Up until now, we've talked about applying styles to items in an iterative process – it doesn't matter how many items feature in our group; each will have the same set of styles applied to them. This demo shows a different way of looping through items; it has one key difference, so let's pause for a moment and reflect on the code from our demo in more detail.

Dissecting the Demo

The @each function is different – as a start, there is no emphasis on numbers; @each will iterate through everything that is included in the targeted list. However, where using @each helps, is in the ability to group properties together for each item in a list; Sass will apply each property to that item in turn.

Take for example our demo – we created a set of three buttons, which had button types and colors applied to them, in pairs:

```
$states: (publish, $publish),
         (postpone, $postpone),
         (delete, $delete);
@each $buttonstate, $color in $states {

   ...


  .#{$buttonstate} {
    ...
    &:hover { background-color: darken( $color, 10% );
      transition: all 0.3s ease; }
```

```
    &:active { background: darken($color,25%); }
  }
}
```

We started by creating a list of items for each button – the list items are in pairs, with $buttonstate and $color values assigned to each button. We then iterate through each pairing, using string interpolation to create styles based on the button type. At the same type, we create hover and active states for each button, using the supplied $color value which is darkened by 10% for hover and 25% for active states respectively.

Looping if a Condition Is True

On occasions we may not have a defined number of items to iterate through, or that this number may vary – in these instances using a @for loop or @each in an array will not work. Instead, we must use another function – @while.

So – I hear you ask: What's the difference? Well, the answer is simple – it works on the basis that it will keep loop *while a given condition can be met.* The moment we can't satisfy this condition, then the loop will stop, and Sass will move on to compile the next set of rules in the style sheet. In many cases, a @while loop works in much the same way as other languages such as JavaScript – to see what I mean, let's take a look at a simple example, where we iterate through ten list items, styling each with a darker shade of color.

LOOPING @WHILE TRUE

Our demo is very simple to put together, so let's make a start:

1. We'll begin by downloading a copy of the whileloop folder from the code download that accompanies this book – save it to the root of our project folder.

2. Next, we need to add in our Sass styling – for this, go ahead
    and create a new file, saving it as `whileloop.scss` in the
    `sass` subfolder in the condition folder we saved in step 1.

3. We have a few style rules to add in, which we will add in block by
    block, starting with some basic styles required to set up our demo:

```scss
$start-color: gainsboro;
$end-color: black;
$white: #ffffff;

$step: 1; // Set the initial step value

@font-face {
  font-family: 'pt_sansregular';
  src: url('../font/pt_sansregular.woff') format('woff');
  font-weight: normal;
  font-style: normal;
}

body { font-family: 'pt_sansregular', sans-serif;
margin: 32px; padding: 32px 80px; width: 550px; }
```

4. We're creating a set of list items, so for this we need to apply
    some basic styling that is common to each list item, such as
    font size:

```scss
ul { margin: 0; padding: 0; }

li {
  color: $white;
  display: inline-block;
  font-size: 24px;
  list-style-type: none;
  margin-bottom: 3.2px;
  padding: 8px;
  width: 80px;
}
```

5. The last part of our Sass styling takes care of applying an increasingly darker shade of color to each list item:

```
@while $step <=10  {
  // changes from one color to another
  .mix li:nth-child(#{$step}) {
    background-color: mix($end-color, $start-color,
    ($step * 10));
  }

  $step: $step + 1;
}
```

6. Go ahead and save the file – next, fire up a terminal session and change the working folder to the whileloop folder under our project area.

7. At the prompt, type the following command and press Enter:

```
sass sass\whileloop.scss css\whileloop.css
```

8. If all is well, we should see a whileloop.css file appear in the css folder, along with a source map – previewing the results will show a simple template page with styled elements, as indicated in Figure 4-9.

Introducing Dart SASS: Mixing Colors in a While Loop

| Item 1 | Item 2 | Item 3 | Item 4 | Item 5 |
| Item 6 | Item 7 | Item 8 | Item 9 | Item 10 |

Figure 4-9. Styling list items using a while loop

When working with multiple items of the same type, using a loop is a great way to apply styles iteratively, without the need to write out style declarations for each item individually. This is a useful technique to learn, even if it is not one you might use immediately when starting with Sass – let's take a moment to explore how our code works in more detail.

Exploring the Code in Detail

So – how does our code work? Well, most of the style declarations are standard CSS – the key to making our demo work lies in this function:

```
@while $step <=10  {
  // changes from one color to another
  .mix li:nth-child(#{$step}) {
    background-color: mix($end-color, $start-color, ($step * 10));
  }

  $step: $step + 1;
}
```

In this code, we create a loop, with a variable $step set to an (implied) value of zero. We then use this value to replace the code highlighted in bold (an interpolated string), to create our rule – this rule contains a declaration for background-color, which is a mix of two colors (gainsboro – or very light gray - and black). We then round out the loop by increasing the value of $step by 1 – this moves us onto the next list item in the group. We can see the effects of this function in the example code shown in Figure 4-10.

```
.mix li:nth-child(3) {                    whileloop.scss:38
    background-color: ■#9a9a9a;
}

li {                                       whileloop.scss:26
    color: □#ffffff;
    display: inline-block;
    font-size: 24px;
    list-style-type: none;
    margin-bottom: 3.2px;
    padding: ▸ 8px;
    width: 80px;
}
```

Figure 4-10. *Compiled code from a @while loop*

See how easy that was to style each item? Granted, our code is probably a little over-simplistic, but the same principle of repeatability applies here too – as long as we have a suitable group of elements (such as list items), we can then use Sass to apply styles to each automatically.

Okay – let's move on: it's time to turn our attention to a more recent addition to Sass. When styling elements, we might create a "palette" of styles that should be kept for certain elements, such as headings or tables. Instead of creating a host of different variables, we can use a more efficient process: we can create a map. Okay – I don't mean trying to replicate cartographers have been doing for years, but something different: a way of referring to particular properties that have been grouped together. Let's dive in and take a look to see what this means in practice.

Applying Styles to a Property List or Map

Although Sass maps are a relatively new concept to Sass (having been introduced in version 3.3 of Ruby Sass, the predecessor to Dart Sass), it is worth its weight in gold – why? Well, let me explain how they work:

Historically, we would likely have created multiple variables to store values – this works, but is a very manual, inefficient way to store values: in addition, we can't really group each item, save for where they might appear in a style sheet.

Instead, we can use a map – these consist of a minimum of two parts: the initial map variable and the block where we call each reference. In the single variable, we can assign multiple key pairings, using this syntax:

```
$map: (key1: value1, key2: value2, key3: value3);
```

... where the key is the map reference, and the value is the attribute we want to display in our style sheet at compilation. When we need to call a value, we would use something akin to this:

```
text-align: map-get(<name of map reference, or key>, <property from that map>)
```

Let's put this into practice, by revisiting one of my favorite effects – we'll style an image of a vintage camera, using the classic Polaroid effect.

CREATING AND USING SASS MAPS

For this next demo, we'll use a premade demo that already uses Sass but which can easily be converted to use a Sass map. Our vintage camera image was sourced from the Pexels website at `https://www.pexels.com/photo/antique-camera-classic-lens-242433/`.

Let's update the demo to use a Sass map:

1. We'll begin by downloading a copy of the `sassmap` folder from the code download that accompanies this book – save it to the root of our project folder.

2. This time around, our demo already has Sass styling, but we're going to modify it – for this, open the `sassmap.scss` file in the sass subfolder in the `sassmap` folder we saved in step 1.

3. At the top of the file, go ahead and insert this, before the
    opening @font-face declaration:

```
$styling-figcaption: (
    'text-align': center,
    'font-family': Reenie Beanie,
    'font-size': 20.8px,
    'color': #454f40,
    'letter-spacing': 1.44px,
);
```

4. Scroll down until you see figcaption{, on or around line 69.

5. Go ahead and replace the contents of this style rule, so it looks
    like this:

```
figcaption {
    text-align: map-get($styling-figcaption, 'text-align');
    font-family: map-get($styling-figcaption, 'font-family');
    font-size: map-get($styling-figcaption, 'font-size');
    color: map-get($styling-figcaption, 'color');
    letter-spacing: map-get($styling-figcaption, 'letter-
    spacing');
}
```

6. Go ahead and save the file – next, fire up a terminal session
    and change the working folder to the sassmap folder under our
    project area.

7. At the prompt, type the following command and press Enter:

```
sass sass\sassmap.scss css\sassmap.css
```

8. If all is well, we should see a sassmap.css file appear in the
    css folder, along with a source map – previewing the results
    will show a simple template page with styled elements, as
    indicated in Figure 4-11.

Introducing Dart Sass: Creating Sass Maps

Figure 4-11. *Creating a Polaroid image using a map*

A really simple change to make, but one which makes our code infinitely easier to manage – not only can we now access each property from a single variable, we can do so multiple times throughout our code. We've only scratched the surface of how maps work in Sass, though: there is a lot more we can do! Nevertheless, it's worth spending a moment going through our code, to see just how powerful maps really are in Sass development.

Breaking Down Our Code

At first glance, our updated code may look more "wordy" (i.e., there is more code there than previously). However, bear in mind that Sass often has instances where this is the case – in this case, it's all about making it easier to get a sense of which value we are using in our code.

Our code starts by adding in a map, which is a group of paired properties; this is assigned to a single variable. Think of it as an array, for those of you who are familiar with this technique; it works in much the same way. Maps are perfect for grouping together common styles for particular elements on a page, such as titles or an <h2> tag.

We then make reference to this map when we create the `figcaption` rule – instead of entering the values directly into the rule, we simply replace them with calls to the `$styling-figcaption` map, with appropriate references to the attribute we want to retrieve.

The grouping together makes it easier to identify what that property relates to, and eliminates the need for multiple variables in our code. So – for example, if we were to call `map-get($styling-figcaption, 'text-align')`, we would get back center as the attribute. We might have initially set as one of several attributes for titles (as mentioned previously), but we can call this `map-get()` function and use it for any example in our code, not just for titles!

Creating Breakpoints Using @media

Throughout the course of this chapter, we've touched on the various ways we can use Sass functions to perform tasks (such as generating colors), or its control directives to determine what should be written to our style sheet.

There is however one more control directive we've yet to cover – and one which should be instantly recognizable to anyone who has spent time developing for responsive sites. Yes, I am talking about `@media` – this works in much the same way as in standard CSS, with one extra capability: media directives can be nested within Sass content.

Put simply, this means that any which appear in a CSS rule will bubble up to the top level of the style sheet – it makes it easy to add in media-specific styles without having to repeat selectors or wreck the flow of our style sheet. Let's take a look at what this means in practice, with a simple proof of concept to show off how we might implement media directives using Sass.

CREATING BREAKPOINTS

For the purposes of this demo, we're going to keep it super simple in terms of elements – we'll have a single <div> that will change color when the screen width has been resized. Let's make a start on setting up our exercise:

1. We'll begin by downloading a copy of the breakpoints folder from the code download that accompanies this book – save it to the root of our project folder.

2. The download contains all of the markup, but this will be useless without our styling, so let's create a new file, saving it as breakpoints.scss in the sass folder for this demo.

3. We have a few style rules to add in, which we will add in block by block, starting with some basic styles required to set up our demo:

```
@font-face {
  font-family: 'pt_sansregular';
  src: url('../font/pt_sansregular.woff') format('woff');
  font-weight: normal;
  font-style: normal;
}

body { font-family: 'pt_sansregular', sans-serif;
margin: 32px; font-size: 20.8px; }
```

4. Next up come the styles required to set our breakpoints – we first set a Sass map to store our breakpoints:

```
$media-queries: (
  tablet: (
    breakpoint: '(min-width: 480px) and (max-width: 768px)',
  ),
```

```
    mobile: (
      breakpoint: '(max-width: 480px)'
    )
  );
```

5. We then need to add in our mixin, which will be called on to
    create our styles:

```scss
@mixin media-query ($size) {
  @each $item, $value in $media-queries {
    @if $item == $size {
      @if map-get($value, breakpoint) != null {
        @media only screen and #{map-get($value,
        breakpoint)} {
          @content;
        }
      }
    }
  }
}
```

6. We're almost done with the styles – last, but by no means least,
    comes the basic style for our responsive <div> element, along
    with the calls to the mixin to add our responsive colors:

```scss
.row { display: inline-block; width: 100%; font-size:
22.4px;
  text-align: center; color: #FFF; padding: 4% 10%; box-
  sizing: border-box; }

.row {
  background: darkgrey;
  @include media-query(mobile) {
    background: lightgrey;
  }
```

```
@include media-query(tablet) {
  background: darkgrey;
}
}
```

7. Go ahead and save the file – next, fire up a terminal session
    and change the working folder to the breakpoints folder
    under our project area.

8. At the prompt, type the following command and press Enter:

    sass sass\breakpoints.scss css\breakpoints.css

9. If all is well, we should see a breakpoints.css file appear
    in the css folder, along with a source map – previewing the
    results will show a simple template page with styled elements,
    as indicated in Figure 4-12.

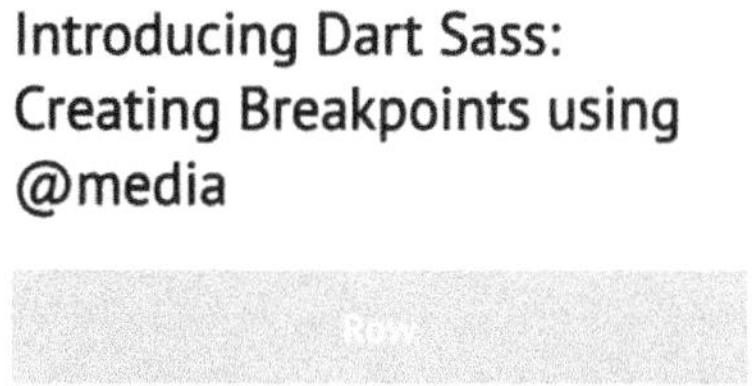

Introducing Dart Sass:
Creating Breakpoints using
@media

Row

Figure 4-12. *Our finished breakpoint example, at table width*

Although our demo only contains one element, there is still a
reasonable amount of code that we've had to add to make it responsive!
Our code shows off some key techniques that are worth mastering; most
of these you have already met earlier in the book, but not in the context of
making elements responsive. Let's take a few minutes to revisit the code to
see how it works in more detail.

Understanding What Happened

Although we've met most of the techniques used in this demo before, at first glance you might be confused for thinking it looks harder than it first appears. In reality, it's fairly straightforward code, so let's go through it step by step:

The real meat of our code starts in step 4, where we've created that map of media breakpoints – we've specified two typical ones (tablet and mobile), but could equally include breakpoints for desktop and other devices as needed. Inside this map, we've specified a breakpoint between 480px and 768px, alongside another to cater to devices no wider than 480px.

Next up we have a mixin – into this we pass the size as a text name, which in this case will be mobile or tablet. We then iterate through each item within the map; if the map contains an item of the right size, we map-get its breakpoint $value, provided a suitable value exists in the map. Assuming such a value exists, then we use the special keyword content to apply this media query across all declarations, right up to the top level of that selector. This will give us something akin to the example shown in Figure 4-13.

```
@media only screen and (max-width: 480px)
.row {                                    breakpoints.scss:45
    background: ▸ ▨ lightgrey;
}

.row {                                    breakpoints.scss:45
    background:▸ ▨ darkgrey;
}
```

Figure 4-13. *Our compiled media query*

Our code looks complex, but in reality, the only parts we need to worry about are the Sass map and calls to the mixin – the mixin itself won't change, and can equally be imported from a separate style sheet using the @include command. This lets us concentrate on providing the right breakpoints for the media query map (which could equally be imported too), and to ensure that calls are positioned at appropriate points in our style sheet.

Summary

Phew – what a ride! We've covered a huge amount of content throughout this chapter, so before we move onto creating the demo in the next chapter, let's take a moment to review what we've learned in this chapter.

We kicked off with a look at using functions within Sass – we saw how these can be used for a variety of purposes but which are particularly suited to tasks such as creating colors. We also explored the benefits of using functions in this manner, and how this makes it easier to create code.

Next up came a look at how we might assign styles at compilation, based on evaluating certain conditions – this included a look at Sass's control directives and expressions, and the various ways we can automate the creation of styles by iterating through groups of elements in a loop. We also took a look at how we can either specify a known number of items in that loop, or use a loop which will only run if certain conditions can be met in our code.

We then moved on to explore the use of Sass maps and saw how easy it is to assign values to a single placeholder, whereas before we might have used multiple variables to perform the same task. We then rounded out the chapter with a brief look at the @media directive, to see how Sass might help with creating media queries for responsive sites or online applications.

Well – we're almost at the end of the book, but we can't leave without putting some of what we've covered thus far into practice! To help with this, we're going to run through a mini case study to see how we might use some of the techniques we've learned in a more practical example – it's time to get those dummy credit cards at the ready, as we're going to create the user interface for a shopping cart. If I were you, I would go get a coffee or drink first, as we have a lot to cover over the next few pages …!

Making the Conversion to Using Sass

Over the course of this book, we've met Sass for the first time and have been introduced to a number of new techniques to help with producing valid CSS code. Much of the code we've written has been from ground up; I suspect that many will ask – how do I convert an existing project to use Sass?

It's a great question: much of what we've learned assumes that in an ideal world, we'd be writing code from scratch, which is the best way to get the most out of Sass. Clearly this perfect scenario doesn't always happen, so we must allow for this in our development. It might seem daunting to convert a monster style sheet into something resembling valid Sass code, but with a little patience and careful planning, it can happen. To help with this, there are three key factors to bear in mind:

- Sass is just a superset of CSS – don't think you have to convert everything in one go! Instead, make your changes in stages: it may take longer but will be more effective longer term.

- Planning and being methodical is absolutely key – make sure your code is consistently formatted: for example, color codes should use the same notation (#fff or #ffffff for white, but not both).

© Alex Libby 2019
A. Libby, *Introducing Dart Sass*, https://doi.org/10.1007/978-1-4842-4372-5_5

- Automate as much as you can – there are tools available to help, such as using Autoprefixer to cater for any vendor prefixes during compilation.

It doesn't matter how long or short a style sheet is – we can use the same techniques to break it down and convert it into its Sass equivalent. Indeed, you may find the longer the better: take, for example, WordPress's own style sheet, which is over 4,500 lines long and is itself written using Sass.

There are a few tricks we can use to help with making the transition to using Sass, so no matter what the project is, let's take a look at how we can make the conversion process easier.

Simplifying the Process

At first glance, converting a monster-sized style sheet will indeed seem daunting – over the course of this chapter, I will show you a number of tips and techniques we can use to make a start on the conversion process, and break it down into more manageable steps.

The first priority, of course, is to get our Sass development workflow set up – we've already used the manual compiler to produce CSS code, but it's likely we will want more; it's time to step things up a notch! It's at this point we will need to automate our process: I would recommend using Node.js, along with some of these tools:

- Autoprefixer for adding vendor prefixes where needed: `https://github.com/postcss/autoprefixer`;

- Image spriting / minifier tools – try this plugin for creating sprites: `https://www.npmjs.com/package/spritesmith`, or `https://www.npmjs.com/package/imagemin` for an image minifier plugin;

- Live-Reload: head over to `https://www.npmjs.com/package/livereload` for a version that works with Node.js;

- A task runner – an optional extra; you can use any such as Gulp (`https://gulpjs.com`) or Grunt (`https://gruntjs.com`), or remain with pure Node.js if preferred;

- Syntax checker for text editor – my personal favorite is Sublime Text (`https://www.sublimetext.com/3`); this has a syntax checker plugin for Sass available from `https://packagecontrol.io/packages/Sass`.

Of course, a lot of what you use will depend on whether you have an existing workflow in place; Sass is one of those libraries that doesn't require a lot of additional tools to get started. Assuming we've set up our development environment, here's a checklist of pointers to help with the initial changes to using Sass:

- Before we make any changes, I would recommend reading the content at `https://sass-guidelin.es/` – written by Hugo Giraudel, this gives some useful tips on how to structure Sass style sheets and code.

- The simplest change we can make is to rename our style sheet to have an `.scss` extension – Sass is just a superset of CSS, so any styles within will compile just fine (and in reality, will be left untouched by the compiler anyway!).

- Consider removing any vendor prefixed versions declarations in your code; this will simplify your code, and these can be added later automatically using the Autoprefixer tool.

- Make sure all of your values are consistently formatted. This will make it easier to replace code when we start to add variables, using the search and replace option in our text editor.

- I would recommend checking and restructuring your code into recognizable sections where possible – this will make it easier to convert into partials, which can be imported during compilation.

- Start reading through your code *carefully* – do you see any repetition in your code, where you're specifying the same values in more than one place?

At this point it's absolutely worth spending time planning how your style sheet will look once converted to Sass. We should make full use of Sass's ability to import multiple files during the compilation process, so common elements can easily be grouped together and stored in individual files.

There is no right or wrong way to how you structure these files; much of it will depend on individual requirements, but over time you will find yourself developing a structure that suits most of the projects you work on when using Sass.

The key to ultimate success, though, will be how your partials are structured – your aim is to separate code into separate files, such that you keep the need for importing files multiple times to a minimum. To give you a flavor of how one might structure folders, you can check out the example given by Danny Huang – for smaller projects, he uses a base file (for most of his code, including resets), a components file (for reusable code such as buttons), and a layout file to handle the overall layout of content. These are all combined into his main file during compilation.

You can read Danny's article on structuring Sass code at
`https://medium.com/@dannyhuang_75970/sass-project-structure-for-big-projects-8c4a740846ee`.

For larger projects, though, this might not be enough – instead, we can use something akin to his model for larger projects:

- base/ - for animations, typography, and utilities

- components/ - stored as single Sass files for each component

- layout/ - used for storing header, grid, footer, and navigation styles

- pages/ - depending on structure, we might have a single Sass file for each page

- abstracts/ - for functions, mixins, and variables

- vendors/ - third-party CSS

- main.scss

It's all about planning – the more you can do now, the easier it will be later! Bear in mind, though: a structure doesn't have to be rigid – we can absolutely develop something to suit projects and modify it if circumstances change.

Okay – let's return to that checklist:

- Assuming you've seen instances of repetition – how much is common between multiple styles? In an ideal world, you're looking for instances where 3–4 declarations are the same (or very close): these could be turned into mixins and these called from within the relevant rules.

- Check items such as buttons, where styles are likely to consist of some common base rules, with only minimal differences such as colors. If this is the case, then consider using the extend function, to reduce duplication of content.

- If you read through your code, do you see instances where you have CSS rules that go several levels deep? A typical example might be within navigation, where you use multiple <li> elements to style each part of an unordered list. Consider converting these to nested styles – it will make it easier to read your content and help cut down on duplication of code.

- A longer-term change you can make is to consider making use of prebuilt libraries where others have already developed code such as mixins or color variables that you can reuse in your code.

- Images – can any be converted to sprites, if you aren't already using them? Sass makes using sprites very easy – it won't suit some of the larger images, but it will be perfect for smaller ones. Alternatively, consider using SVG images for icons – as these are made up of HTML and CSS, they can be styled using Sass with ease, and (depending on how you call them), can also reduce the number of requests we make of our server!

See how easy it is to start using Sass, with just a few changes? Granted, there will be other changes we can make over time, but these will give you a good head start when making the initial change to using Sass as a development tool.

Talking of making changes – we can do these manually (as it gives us a great feel for where we can make them), or we can make use of some conversion tools to do some of the heavy lifting for us. Although these tools may not give us the finished article, they will at least give us a good head start – over the next few pages, we'll take a look at one of these tools in more detail, to see just how they work in action.

Making a Start on Conversion

Okay – so we've talked about how we might approach the conversion process: it's time for action!

When converting Sass, one should always consider it to be an iterative process that evolves over time; the likelihood of us having a really simple style sheet is probably next to zero. We can, of course, try to convert it manually, but this will be a time-consuming process.

Instead, why not put it through one of several tools already available for download, which can do some of the heavy lifting for us? There are a couple of examples available, including css2scss (`https://www.css2scss.com/`), or the css2sass app available at `http://css2sass.herokuapp.com/`.

A personal favorite, though, is the Styleflux tool, which you can install using Node.js from `https://www.npmjs.com/package/styleflux`. Granted, it might not produce perfect results, but as the only cost to using it is a the initial set-up (which only has to be done once), why not give it a try? The worst that can happen is that it falls into a complete heap and produces garbage; in many cases, you will get something respectable, which may only need a little tweaking and tidying up. Let's put this theory to the test, and see how it works, as part of our next demo.

CONVERT TO SASS USING STYLEFLUX

For this exercise, we'll assume you have Node.js installed from Chapter 1 – if you don't, then I would recommend revisiting that chapter for a reminder!

Assuming we have Node.js installed, then we need to follow these steps:

1. We'll start by creating a new folder in our project area – call it css2scss.

2. Next, fire up a Node.js terminal session (not a standard one!), and navigate to our project area.

3. We now need to create a `package.json` file, which Node.js uses to tell it which packages to use – for this, enter the following at a prompt, and press Enter:

```
npm init -y
```

4. When it confirms a `package.json` file has been created, then enter this at the prompt and press Enter:

```
npm install styleflux -save
```

If you get Node complaining of a `package-lock.json` file being created, then you can stop this from happening – copy the `.npmrc` and `.gitignore` files from the code download to the root of the `css2scss` folder.

---

5. Next, we need to create our conversion script – for this, go ahead and add the following code to a new file, saving it as `styleflux.js` in our project area:

```
const cssConverter = require('styleflux');
cssConverter.processCSSFile("test.css");
```

6. We can now test our file conversion – for this, switch back to the terminal session, then make sure the working folder is the `css2scss` folder.

7. At the prompt, enter this command, and press Enter:

```
node styleflux.js
```

8. If all is well, we should see the name of a new file being created with our Sass code, as indicated in Figure 5-1.

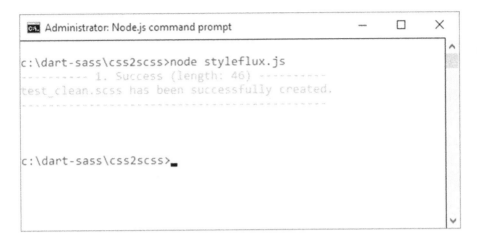

Figure 5-1. *Successful conversion of a CSS file*

As an aside – if you want to try different style sheets, please change the name highlighted in step 5, before running saving the file and running it from step 6 onward.

---

9. Once the file has finished being converted, you will see confirmation posted on screen – go ahead and open the file, which will be in the root of the css2scss folder, to confirm it has indeed produced a workable result.

At this point, I'll bet you'll be asking either one of two questions – how effective is this tool with larger files? And why didn't we simply use it first …? These are equally pertinent questions: the answer to the first might surprise you, and there is a good reason for not simply using the tool outright. Intrigued? Let's dive in and take a look at why. …

Using the css2scss Tool – a Postscript

Anyone who knows me personally will say that I'm a big fan of the KISS principle – for those of you who are unaware, it means keep it simple, stu.....okay, I'll let you fill in the rest!

But seriously though: we live in an age where time is crucial, and I'm all for automating those tasks that are time consuming and add little of value. That said, I've also said we should absolutely read through our code to understand where we can make changes. This would appear to contradict the previous approach, so what gives?

There are several reasons why we should follow both approaches – a conversion tool won't be 100% perfect; it is reliant on us producing code that uses consistent notation, such as using just 6-digit hex codes, or mixing in color names. A read through the code to start with means we can check it for consistency; we can also get a feel for where we will be able to convert it to using Sass. Once this is done, we can then run it through the css2scss tool before checking the results in a text editor.

In terms of how well it works – this might surprise you: while researching for this book, I tested it on a heavy style sheet from the twentyseventeen theme that comes with WordPress. This beast weighs in at around 4,300 lines of code – it certainly is no lightweight. However, it doesn't seem to have caused any issue: the tool converted it with little difficulty, producing a Sass style sheet that weighs in at just under 2,000 lines! It has to be said this would need checking, but it's definitely worth giving it a try, if only to understand more about how we might make the changes manually.

Okay – let's change tack: as part of converting a style sheet to using Sass, we might decide to split it into smaller, more manageable chunks, or partials. There is nothing wrong with this; it's a perfectly acceptable approach.

However, I suspect you may find yourself creating code similar to that created by other developers and who have posted it online – why not have a look? Rather than reinvent the wheel, see what you can find that people may have already created: there are dozens of libraries available online for us to use. I would absolutely recommend taking time to research possible options; who knows what you might find! Making use of prebuilt libraries is not without its issues – to understand why, let's dive in and take a look at what is involved in more detail.

Using a Prebuilt Library

Cast your mind back to our discussion earlier in this chapter, under "Simplifying the Process." Remember how we talked about using the @import function to break down larger style sheets into more manageable chunks?

This is the basic principle of how we create Sass libraries – they are nothing more than smaller files containing code such as mixins, loops, variables, and the like, or even components relating to a specific part of the site (such as navigation). The key though is that if we import the file into our style sheet, Sass will only call code that is directly referenced from the main style sheet.

We can take this a step further – we can, of course, create our own libraries. In some cases, though, there may be no need: others may have done something for us already that we can reuse in our code. Instead of trying to reinvent the wheel, we can simply import their file – Sass will use only those mixins, functions, and the like that are called from our main style sheet, and the rest will be left untouched.

To really understand how this works, let's dive into a demo – it may be somewhat simplistic in nature, but when using @import, it's the *process* that counts, not the end result.

Exploring Prebuilt Options

Process, process – surely the end result is more important, I hear you ask?

Yes – clearly, we want to achieve the right result. However, the means by which we get there is arguably more important. Let me explain what I mean.

If we opt to use a prebuilt library, it's an almost certain that we will find one that contains all of the mixins, variables, or functions that we need for a project. The trick here is to find the ones that strike the right balance of functionality we can use, against options that are of no interest to us (at least for the project in hand).

We can, of course, simply import multiple libraries, but this is inefficient – there is little point importing one if we only use a tiny proportion of the functionality within it. We may also find others at a later date that contain better versions of mixins, or include more functionality within – we can then decide to refactor our code to do away with redundant libraries if we want to use a better option.

This is just a scratch on the surface of what we might have to consider when using @import – we'll come back to this shortly; but for now, let's work through a simple example to show you how we can use @import to reference libraries when working with Sass.

USING A PREBUILT LIBRARY

This demo assumes that you have installed Node.js from Chapter 1, which we need to use to download Bourbon – if you've not already done it, make sure you have installed it, before you continue with this exercise.

Assuming it is in place and working, these are the steps you need to follow:

1. We'll begin by extracting a copy of the library-prebuilt folder from the code download that accompanies this book: go ahead and store it in our project folder.

CHAPTER 5   MAKING THE CONVERSION TO USING SASS

2. We now need to download the Bourbon library, so fire up a Node.js terminal session and change the working folder to the `library-prebuilt` folder in our project area.

3. At the terminal prompt, enter this command and press Enter:

    ```
    npm install bourbon --save
    ```

4. When the download has completed, go ahead and copy the _ bourbon.scss file and bourbon folder from `node_modules\` `bourbon\core` to the sass folder under the `library-prebuilt` folder.

We now have Bourbon in place – if you've gotten this far: well done! It does raise some questions about how we use libraries, but for now, let's update our code to use Bourbon:

5. Go ahead and open `library-prebuilt.scss`, then add this line at the very top of the file:

    ```
    @import "_bourbon.scss";
    ```

6. A little further down, drop this code in place of the comment at line 10:

    ```
    $size: 200px;
    ```

7. On or around line 36, change the declaration for background color to this:

    ```
    background-color: tint(#6ecaa6, 40%);
    ```

8. Save the file, then fire up a terminal session and change the working folder to the `library-prebuilt` folder under our project area.

9. At the prompt, type the following command and press Enter:

    ```
    sass sass\skeleton.scss css\skeleton.css
    ```

10.   If all is well, we should see a `library-prebuilt.css` file appear in the `css` folder, along with a source map – previewing the results will show a simple template page with styled elements, as indicated in Figure 5-2.

Introducing Dart SASS: Migrating to using a SASS Library

Figure 5-2. *Switching to use a prebuilt library*

At face value, the steps we've worked through in this demo are relatively straightforward – they illustrate the kind of changes we might have to make to existing Sass code, if we decide to switch to using a prebuilt library of some description. However, I intimated that this is just a small part of the overall process – there are some key points we should be aware of when using `@import`, so let's dive in and find out how these might affect our development.

Assessing the Pitfalls – a Postscript

If you plug in the phrase "sass code libraries" into a browser, you will get dozens of results – some will be reviews of libraries, or you may see links for individual sites such as Bourbon (`https://bourbon.io`) and Saffron (`http://colindresj.github.io/saffron/`), or some of the lesser-known ones such as Sassmatic (`http://sassmatic.com/`) or Scut (`http://davidtheclark.github.io/scut/`).

Trouble is – how to decide which one to use? It's a good question: this is one process that takes time, patience, and lots of testing before you find the right answer! To help with the process, there are a few tips I can recommend:

- Have a good look online at articles where people have selected libraries for review – you may find some names appearing mo re than once, which is a good indicator of their popularity. Alternatively look for curated lists such as the one at `https://github.com/Famolus/awesome-sass` – this will contain some useful starting links, although some may now be out of date!

- Many libraries are open source – this means that while others may have contributed fixes and improvements, there will not likely be any form of formal support offer in place. It means you will be reliant on the goodwill of others to help resolve problems, and that there is no guarantee a fix will be implemented quickly if you have a time-sensitive issue! This may not be a problem, but it is something to bear in mind.

- On a more serious note, as Dart Sass is still relatively new, you will find that many libraries still refer to the older Ruby method of installing them. This isn't necessary, but it does mean you may be limited in terms of which library you use, or how you install it – not every library may have versions available for NPM, Yarn, or the like.

- You may find people have created libraries that offer mixins that cater to your need, but which work slightly differently to achieve the same result – bear in mind that you may have to adapt your code first to match it, **before** you switch to using the prebuilt version.

- Although Sass will only use import mixins where they are directly referenced in code, there is little benefit in referencing a large library for a small amount of code, such as one or two mixins only! In this case, it's better to copy them into your own library – it will make it easier to manage and keep the compilation times down.

- Many libraries contain mixins solely for the purpose of providing vendor support, which isn't necessary, for all but the newest of CSS properties. We can use a tool such as Autoprefixer during compilation (although this will require Node.js) – this tool will take care of vendor prefixes automatically. A good example of this are the mixins provided by the Compass library at http://www.compass-style.org, for properties such as background-clip; this is now supported without the need for vendor prefixes.

- Consider this as an evolving process – it's rare that you will find all of the mixins, functions, variables, and the like already in a prebuilt library. You may need to go through several iterations of libraries before you find the right combination that best serves the needs of your project.

These are just a few of the considerations we will likely need to bear in mind when choosing prebuilt libraries – hopefully you will see that the process of choosing is just as important as the end result, if not more so!

Whichever library (or libraries) you choose to use in your project, there is one thing that we absolutely must do: ensure our import process has been optimized. Optimization can mean the difference between compiling concise code and code with hundreds of extra lines of bloat – clearly not something we need. It's a key part of importing, so let's dive in and see what this means in practice for us.

Optimizing the Import Process

Over the last few pages, we've talked about importing files, and how this powerful tool can really help with managing your style sheets – instead of having to try to manage a monster file as one, we can break it down into smaller, more manageable chunks that make it easier to maintain.

There is a risk, though, when using the @import function – if we're not careful about how we structure it, we can end up creating more styles than intended! For a small project, this is less of an issue; but, for larger ones, this could have a real impact on speed, particularly if our browser has to wade through hundreds of extra lines of code that are redundant.

To understand what an impact this can have, we're going to turn our attention to a small demo – the main style sheet only has three style rules within it, but as you will shortly see, this is not what we get once our file is compiled. ...

CARELESS IMPORTING

I have a small confession to make – I am sure the title of this demo will not apply to you, but once you've seen the result of this demo, I'm sure you will understand the significance! With that in mind, let's make a start on our demo:

1. We'll begin by extracting a copy of the import-original file from the code download that accompanies this book – go ahead and save it in our project area.

2. Next, open your text editor, and add the following code to a new file, saving it as font-sizes.scss in our project folder:

```
$h1-size: 36px;
$h2-size: 24px;
$h3-size: 18px;
```

```
$grey: #212121;
$lightgrey: #616161;

.h1 {
  color: $grey;
  font-size: $h1-size;
}

.h2 {
  color: $grey;
  font-size: $h2-size;
}

.h3 {
  color: $lightgrey;
  font-size: $h3-size;
}

.copy {
  color: $grey;
  font-size: $h3-size * 0.5;
}
```

3. We need to add one more file – for this, add the following styles to a new file, saving it as page.scss in our project folder:

```
@import "font-sizes";

.page_title { @extend .h1; }

.page_cta { @extend .h3; }

.page_special_button { background-color: black; color: white; }
```

4. Fire up a terminal session, then change the working folder to the import-original folder we created in step 1.

5. At the prompt, enter this command, and press Enter:

```
sass page.scss css\page.css
```

6. If we look inside the css folder, we should see two files –
   page.css and page.css.map; these contain our compiled
   styles. Don't open the file just yet – we will do that in a
   moment!

At this point we should have a compiled style sheet in the css folder – before you open the file up, any idea on how many rules you would expect to see? If the answer is three, then I am sorry to disappoint – the true answer is five with two shared rules, as indicated in Figure 5-3.

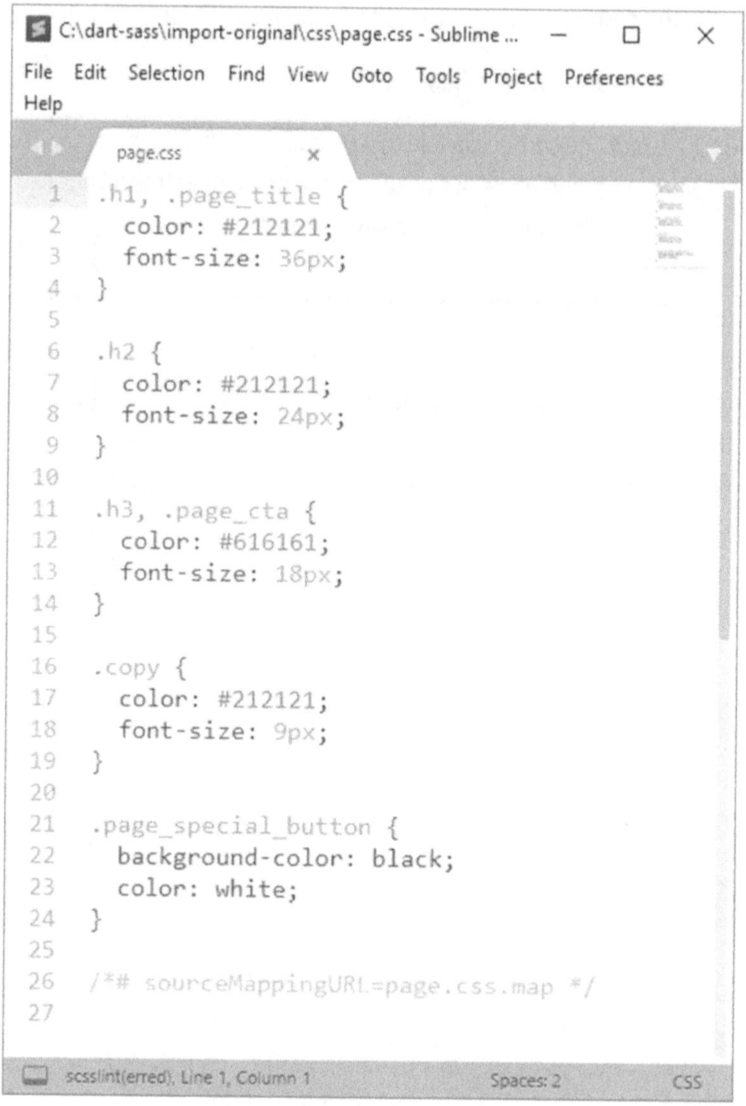

Figure 5-3. *The results of not properly importing files*

Ouch – our style sheet has nearly doubled! We originally wanted three compiled styles, but thanks to how we've set up our style sheet, Sass has treated the extra code as additional style rules and added them during compilation.

The real irony though is that the cause of these extra styles appearing is down to one character that is repeated multiple times in this style sheet, but which forces Sass to add these extra styles during compilation. Yes – the humble full stop is to blame; just like in normal punctuation, its position can make a real difference!

DEMO – OPTIMIZED IMPORTING

Fortunately, we can make a simple change to our code to cure this problem – let's make a start on updating our demo:

1. We'll begin by extracting a copy of the import-optimized file from the code download that accompanies this book – go ahead and save it in our project area.

2. Next, open font-sizes.scss in your text editor – change the full stops on lines 7, 12, 17, and 22 to a % sign, so the start of the code looks similar to this example:

```
%h1 {
  color: $grey;
  ...
```

3. We also need to update page.scss to use the renamed placeholders – for this go ahead and change the full stop in lines 4 and 8 to a % sign, similar to this:

```
.page_title {
  @extend %h1;
}
```

4. Fire up a terminal session, then change the working folder to the import-original folder we created in step 1.

5. At the prompt, enter this command, and press Enter:

```
sass page.scss css\page.css
```

6. If we look inside the css folder, we should see two new files – page.css and page.css.map; these contain our updated styles.

Now – remember what we did at the end of the previous exercise? This time around, we won't have the same six rules we had before – instead, we'll have just three, which is what we would expect to see in our finished article.

At this point, go ahead and open the finished style sheet that you will see as page.css in the css subfolder – inside we can indeed see just three rules, as indicated in Figure 5-4.

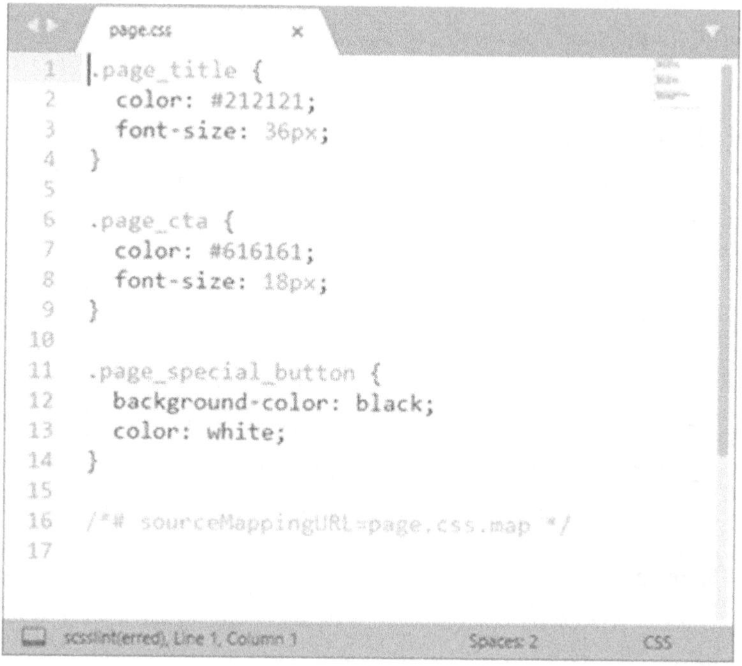

Figure 5-4. *The results of our optimized file*

See how much of a difference a single character can make? This raises two important points about optimizing our code, which will help reduce duplication and bloat – let's take a look at these in more detail.

Understanding the Changes

If we take a look back at the original version of the compiled code, we were expecting to see three rules, but instead got five (with two sharing the same rule).

The reason for this lies in the use of the full stop in the `font-sizes.scss` file (and subsequent references to the styles from the `page.scss` file). This forces Sass to treat them as new styles that should be imported – notice how, for example, that there isn't a reference to `.copy` in `page.scss`, but this is still imported into the final result?

When we changed the full stop over to a percentage sign in the `font-sizes.scss` file, we told Sass that those styles should not be imported as styles in their own right, but only import the content of each style *where it is directly referenced* from an @extend statement in the calling file. This is why when we look at the compiled result for the optimized version, we only see references to `.page_cta`, `.page_title`, and `.page_special_button` - the `.copy` rule, for example, is not referenced in an @extend, so will not appear in this version of the style sheet.

The use of the percentage sign is one way we can use to reduce code bloat – the other lies in the order of how we import our partials, and what is stored within each partial. Take a look at `font-sizes.scss` again: notice how we have variables and style rule declarations within the same file?

In our small example, this works fine, but it could well lead to duplication in more complex style sheets. A better option is to keep all variables in one file only – importing this file early in the list will make variables available globally, as in this example:

```
@import 'base/reset';

@import 'helpers/variables';
@import 'helpers/mixins';
@import 'helpers/functions';
@import 'helpers/helpers';
@import 'helpers/placeholders';

@import 'base/typography';

@import 'pages/versions';
@import 'pages/recording';
@import 'pages/lists';
@import 'pages/global';

@import 'forms/buttons';
@import 'forms/inputs';
@import 'forms/validators';
@import 'forms/fieldsets';

@import 'sections/header';
@import 'sections/navigation';
@import 'sections/sidebar-a';
@import 'sections/sidebar-b';
@import 'sections/footer';

@import 'vendors/ui-grid';

@import 'components/modals';
@import 'components/tooltip';
@import 'components/tables';
@import 'components/datepickers';
```

It may seem a lot of files, but it is important to remember that splitting content into smaller files will make it easier to manage them, as long as we maintain a suitable order. The above list can then be stored in the main style sheet while you work on each partial as needed – Sass will import them all to produce the final version during compilation.

You may see that other developers use the underscore to denote a Sass partial file – this is not obligatory, as Sass will work just fine without them.

Okay – it's time to move on: we've talked a lot about the importance of importing content; time for a little action, methinks! To help really understand how we can use importing, we're going to work on a large CSS style sheet as a real-world example, and transform the content into something more manageable for future development.

Working Through an Example

Remember how I said earlier that you would be unlikely to get much benefit from using @import in a small style sheet, and that the larger the style sheet, the better? It doesn't matter how large the style sheet is – the same principles we've talked about will still apply, although we'll get more benefit from converting a large style sheet than a smaller one.

A great example of a large style sheet is from the TwentySeventeen theme that comes with the self-hosted version of WordPress. The style sheet for this theme is a real monster: it comes in at over 4,000 lines!

It may seem like a daunting task to convert a file of this size, but I will show you that with some care and planning, we will begin to tame this beast into something more manageable. There are, however, a couple of good reasons for picking WordPress's style sheet as the basis for what will be our next exercise:

- WordPress's style sheet was originally created using Sass – it makes it a natural choice.

- Size should not matter: WordPress's style sheet already has comment blocks to split content. This makes it a cinch to convert the file, one block at a time. It's just a matter of planning what is changed and when we make the change.

- If we take a closer look at the code within, WordPress's style sheet contains plenty of examples of declarations that can be converted. A good example would include font names, colors, and sizes that can all be transformed into suitably named variables.

To prove that we can bring a large style sheet under control, no matter the size, we're going to dive in to our next exercise, and do just that: we'll use the aforementioned TwentySeventeen theme, and begin to convert it into something that is easier for us to manage.

REFACTORING WORDPRESS

For this exercise, we'll need a copy of the self-hosted version of WordPress – you can download it from WordPress's website at https://wordpress. org/latest.zip (Windows) or https://wordpress.org/latest.tar. gz (Linux and MacOS). The current version at the time of writing is 4.9.8, although we can apply the same principles to any WordPress theme.

Let's make a start:

1. First, we need to create a working folder for our conversion – save it as theme under our project area.

2.   Next, go ahead and extract a copy of the style sheet – you will find it in the twentyseventeen theme folder, which is under /wordpress/wp-content/themes. I would recommend taking two copies: save one in a new folder called original (under wordpress), and the second in the root of the wordpress folder; rename this second one to style.scss.

3.   Have a look through, then choose a section to work on – I'll assume you've chosen 18.0 SVGs Fallbacks, as it is nice and small; please alter accordingly if you decide to go with a different section.

4.   Within our wordpress folder, create a new folder called fallback. Create a new file within it, saving it as fallback.scss.

5.   Next, open a copy of style.scss, then look for section 18 – it will be around line 3149 onward. Copy and paste all lines from that section into the fallback.scss file and save it.

6.   Revert back to style.scss, then remove the original lines from this section (around lines 3149 to 3206).

7.   In its place, add this code, on line 3149:

```
@import "fallback/svg.scss"
```

8.   Go ahead and save both style.scss and fallback.scss.

9.   Fire up a terminal session, then change the working folder to the wordpress folder we created in step 1.

10. At the prompt, enter this command, and press Enter:

```
sass style.scss csss\style.css
```

11. If we look inside the css folder, we should see two new files – style.css and style.css.map; these contain our updated styles.

12. Open the compiled file and press Ctrl+F to search for "18.0 SVGs Fallbacks"; you should see our fallback block has been recompiled into our master style sheet.

Notice how the code doesn't look any different, but you can now manage it in smaller files? The real test though will come if we were to fire up a copy of WordPress with that theme activated; a successful test will be that we see no apparent changes in the theme, even though it has been compiled using Sass.

If you compare a copy of the original style sheet (in the original folder I hope you created in step 2) with the recompiled version, you may see comments have been removed, but otherwise the CSS should be the same. This is a good indicator that the conversion process will have been successful, and that our theme will continue to function as prior to the change.

Assuming this initial change was successful, this is just the start of our journey into converting the file – there still more we can do! To give you a flavor of what is possible, let's dive in and take a look at our initial change in more detail, along with some suggestions on where we can convert our theme to use Sass.

Exploring the Changes and More in Detail

It may seem like we had a fair few steps to work through, but in reality, we can simplify it by making the compilation process automatic – the addition of the --watch switch at the end of the code in step 10 will suffice. Much of what we do though will be a simple cut-and-paste job, as long as we do it section by section (adding the relevant import statement after each). The key is to be methodical and remain focused – it's too easy to get distracted when converting code!

Now – how about continuing with those changes? We could work through these on our own, but as it so happens, there is a version available online that has already been converted to use Sass.

The code is hosted on GitHub and was created by the developer Jim Frenette; you can see it at `https://github.com/jimfrenette/twentyseventeen-sass`.

I would absolutely encourage you though to try converting the style sheet first yourself though – there is no fun in getting the answer without at least giving it a try! With this in mind, I'm going to pick out a few examples of what can be changed with little difficulty:

- I would recommend adding a `variables.scss` file – this could be saved into a folder called base, then imported using `@import "base/variables.scss"` at the top of your style sheet. This would be for storing all your initial variables, such as colors, font families, or font sizes.

- We can then make use of this variables file – for example, take a look at section 10, which takes care of styling links. The first few lines look like this:

```
a {
  color: #222;
  text-decoration: none;
}

a:focus {
    outline: thin dotted;
}

a:hover,
a:active {
  color: #000;
  outline: 0;
}
```

We can convert them to this – it uses nesting and variables (hence creating the variables.scss file first!):

```scss
a {
  color: $black2;
  text-decoration: none;
  &:focus {
    outline: thin dotted;
  }
  &:hover, &:active {
    color: $black1;
    outline: 0;
  }
}
```

- Take, for example, section 11 – Featured Image Hover; this could easily be converted to look like this:

```scss
/*------------------------------------------------------
11.0 Featured Image Hover
----------------------------------------------------*/

.post-thumbnail {
  margin-bottom: 1em;
  a {
    img {
      -webkit-backface-visibility: hidden;
      transition: opacity 0.2s;
    }
    &:hover img, &:focus img {
      opacity: 0.7;
    }
  }
}
```

- A little more complicated, but something to try: how about a mixin to convert font sizes to their rem unit equivalents? WordPress makes use of both pixel and rem values – a mixin such as this will take care of this:

```
// usage, x is the pixel size needed: @include font-size(x);
@mixin font-size($sizeValue: 15) {
  font-size: $sizeValue + px;
  font-size: ($sizeValue / 16) + rem;
}
```

- So – where we might have something like this in the style sheet:

```
.pagination, .comments-pagination {
  border-top: 1px solid $silver2;
  font-size: 14px;
  font-size: 0.875rem;
  font-weight: 800;
  padding: 2em 0 3em;
  text-align: center;
}
```

... we can update it to use a mixin to provide the font sizes automatically and avoid the need to calculate the relevant sizes manually:

```
.pagination, .comments-pagination {
  @include font-size(14);
  border-top: 1px solid $silver2;
  font-weight: 800;
  padding: 2em 0 3em;
  text-align: center;
}
```

167

These are just a few of the example changes we can make to our style sheet – in each instance, I've tried to keep it simple for now, but as you get more used to making the changes, I am sure you will find others that are more complex and require more work! The trick though is to remain methodical throughout – treat it as an evolving exercise that will require a few iterations before you reach the completed solution.

Summary

Managing styles is clearly an important part of building any online-based project – it's unlikely that we'll ever have a really small site; it's more probable that we'll have a lengthy style sheet that will soon collapse into chaos without careful management! Over the course of this chapter, we've covered some useful tricks to help make Sass-based style sheets easier to manage – let's take a moment to review what we've covered in this chapter.

We kicked off with an introduction to how we might begin to convert an existing project to use Sass – we explored some of the key points that we need to bear in mind, before making a start on a first-pass type transformation, using one of the conversion tools available online.

Next up, we moved to how we might begin to break down our code into smaller, more manageable chunks, and that as part of this, we may make use of external libraries to help cut down the development time. We explored some of the pitfalls we might encounter when using this approach, and how with careful management we can begin to transform our code into something that is easier to manage.

We then moved onto covering an important part of importing libraries – the optimization process, where we learned two key tricks to help get started with getting used to optimizing our code. We then rounded out the chapter with a real-world example of converting a large style sheet into something we can use with Sass, and learned how no matter what the size of the style sheet, we can still make use of some basic principles to convert it to using Sass.

We're almost at the end of this book, but before we reach that point, it's time to get stuck into a real project! There are countless uses for Sass – pretty much wherever we might have CSS, Sass can be used. Over the course of the next chapter, we're going to bring together some of skills we've covered over the course of this book and use them to create something that we'll see on any e-commerce-based site – a shopping cart. Ready to make a start ...?

CHAPTER 6

Introducing Our Project

Over the course of this book, we've introduced a host of different features of Sass and begun to explore how we might make use of them in our projects. The real test, though, comes when we start to tie everything together and begin to build something more practical. The question is – what should we build?

Well, coming from an e-commerce background, it makes sense to investigate building something e-commerce related, right? After all, e-commerce (according to a study by eMarketeer in 2016), is expected to experience double-digit growth until 2020 – with sales estimated to top 27 trillion dollars! I think the phrase "no-brainer" comes to mind...

If you would like to learn more, the report is available on the eMarkeeter website, at `https://bit.ly/2b9RZHd`.

That aside, over the next few pages, we will indeed focus on an e-commerce-related theme – we're going to mock up a demo shopping cart. For reasons of space, we'll focus more on the Sass styling (as it is, of course, the theme for this book); we will touch on some of the HTML markup and JavaScript used to power the site. With this in mind, let's make a start on setting up our cart – we'll begin with a look at setting up our development environment and getting the HTML markup in place.

Setting Up Our Initial Cart

In the age of the Internet, it doesn't seem sensible to try to reinvent the wheel, right? There are dozens of examples of carts available online, all of which have their own features, and which use a variety of technologies to power the cart.

For the purposes of this demo, I've elected to base ours on one created by Žiga Miklič, which uses plain HTML markup along with standard CSS and jQuery to power the site. Our version will have been converted to use Sass; I've also simplified the look and feel and updated the CSS to remove some of the outdated vendor prefixes. This will have the added benefit of showing you how one might convert an existing site to using Sass, rather than building a solution from scratch.

You can see the original version of this cart at `https://codepen.io/ziga-miklic/pen/xhpob`.

Okay – the first stage is to get our markup in place and set up our compilation process. For this demo, we'll use Node.js – this is not only for the purposes of compiling Sass, but to also add a source map (to translate our compiled CSS into the equivalent source location in the Sass code). We'll also make use of Autoprefixer to add in any vendor prefixes automatically – there shouldn't be any now, but it is nevertheless preferred practice when working with Sass.

GETTING SET UP

Assuming Node.js is installed, let's make a start:

1. We'll start by extracting a copy of the `shoppingcart` folder – go ahead and save it locally in our project folder. This contains our markup (`shoppingcart.html`), along with the requisite font, image, and JavaScript files needed for our demo.

2. Next, fire up a Node.js terminal session as administrator, and change the working folder to the `shoppingcart` folder we saved in step 1.

3. Start a Node.js terminal session, then at the prompt enter this command and press Enter: `npm install` – this will install a number of packages using the supplied `package.json` file:

    - Gulp – for automating tasks,

    - Autoprefixer (for Gulp) – for handling any vendor prefixes,

    - Dart Sass,

    - Sourcemaps for Gulp – to provide source maps for translating compiled CSS into the relevant source Sass code.

Re install required – it might show a few warnings, but these can be ignored for the purposes of this demo.

---

4. Once installation has completed, enter `gulp` at the prompt and press Enter.

5. If no errors are displayed, then you can close the terminal session for now.

At this point the Gulp task will run but we won't get anything to appear in the `css` folder – don't worry: it might seem a little odd to do this, but it's purely to prove that our compilation process is working! There are a couple of points of note here, though, so before we move onto setting up our style sheet, let's pause for a moment to understand the initial setup in more detail.

Understanding What Has Happened

Over the course of this book, we've primarily used the command line to compile Sass; in many cases, this is perfectly adequate. However, it becomes tedious as we must run the compilation process manually – we can use the --watch facility to automate compilation, but it is still a stand-alone process!

It's for this reason that we've selected to use Node.js and Gulp (as a task runner) – the latter can be used to automate dozens of different tasks, leaving us to concentrate on developing our code. In our case, we've used a package.json file to tell Node.js to install Gulp, Autoprefixer (for vendor prefix support), source map support, and of course Dart Sass. It's worth noting that we could use a different task runner such as Grunt or even Broccoli – this is just a matter of personal preference; each will work in a similar manner.

Note – in this demo, Gulp was installed for use within the project folder by default; you may prefer to install it globally, particularly if you've already used it previously. For details on how to do this, please refer to the "Automating the Process" demo in Chapter 1 of this book.

For the moment, our project only has a few packages tied into the compilation process – this is to keep things simple for now, but we can easily develop this into something more comprehensive. We might, for example, install a CSS linting tool such as Stylelint (https://stylelint.io), or an image spriting tool (such as Spritesmith, available from https://github.com/twolfson/gulp.spritesmith). The key though being that as long as we consider which steps should come in which order, then we can begin to automate some of those tasks that have less value, but which are clearly a necessary part of developing our projects.

Okay – let's move on: hopefully you didn't see any errors at the end of the previous exercise? Assuming we didn't, then we can continue with the next section of our demo: adding the all-important styles for our cart.

Preparing Our Style Sheet

Yes: it's time to start making our demo look presentable! We'll break this into three parts – the first will take care of some simple font declarations, with part two focusing on declaring variables, and the final part creating the main style sheet.

We'll start by setting up our font declarations: they are not obligatory for the demo, but including them is a useful way to show how we might import such styles into our project when using Sass.

The fonts we'll make use of are PT Sans and Open Sans – they are included in the code download that accompanies this book, or you can download them from the FontSquirrel website at `https://www.fontsquirrel.com/fonts/pt-sans` and `https://www.fontsquirrel.com/fonts/open-sans` respectively. Let's crack on with the demo.

PREPARING THE FONTS

We'll start with the simplest part of our Sass style sheet – setting up the font declarations. This we will do as a separate file or partial, which we will import into the main style sheet during compilation:

1. In a new file, go ahead and add the following declaration for the PT Sans font – this is primarily for the exercise title:

```
@font-face {
  font-family: 'pt_sansregular';
  src: url('../font/pt_sansregular.woff') format('woff');
  font-weight: normal;
  font-style: normal;
}
```

2. Next, leave a line, then add the following three declarations for the Open Sans font – these are used in various places throughout the cart:

```
@font-face {
  font-family: 'open_sanslight';
  src: url('../font/openSans-light-webfont.woff')
  format('woff');
  font-weight: normal;
  font-style: normal;
}

@font-face {
  font-family: 'open_sansregular ';
  src: url('../font/openSans-regular-webfont.woff')
  format('woff');
  font-weight: normal;
  font-style: normal;
}

@font-face {
  font-family: 'open_sansbold';
  src: url('../font/openSans-bold-webfont.woff')
  format('woff');
  font-weight: normal;
  font-style: normal;
}
```

3. Save the file as _fonts.scss within the sass folder – you can close the file for now, but we will revisit it later at the compilation stage.

We now have the first of our import files in place – we aren't done though with imports! We have a second file to set up, which will contain values declared as variables that we will use in our main style sheet. In addition, this imported file will make use of several Sass functions – we'll go into detail shortly, but for now, let's dive in and set up the variables.

You may have noticed the use of the underscore in the `fonts.scss` filename – this is optional; it's a good way to tell if you're working with a partial or the main style sheet. It can be omitted if you prefer to use a more conventional naming format.

Assigning Our Variables

This file is probably the most important out of all three of the style sheet files we create in this demo – it contains all of the values we use, assigned as variables. Without it, our demo will clearly look like rubbish when the code is compiled! This import contains all of the colors defined for our demo, along with declarations for font attributes.

INITIALIZING OUR VARIABLES

Let's make a start on setting up our file:

1. In a new file, add the following block of variables – this takes care of defining some of the base colors we'll use in our demo:

```
$color-black: #000000;
$color-yellow: #ffdb4d;
$color-pure-red: #ff0000;
```

2. Next up, leave a line, then add the following lines of code – these colors are for the remove hover link over the book and the main checkout button:

```
// Cyans
$color-dark-cyan: #429188;
$color-moderate-cyan: lighten(saturate($color-dark-cyan,
2.40), 10.39);
```

3. Leave a line blank, then add the following lines of code – they take care of the background colors within each book article:

```
// Whites
$color-white: #ffffff;
$color-almost-white: darken($color-white, 1.18);
```

4. This last group of colors will be used primarily for borders and as a background color for the total value:

```
// Greys
$color-light-grey: #eeeeee;
$color-description-grey: darken($color-light-grey, 13.33);
$color-very-light-grey: darken($color-light-grey, 7.06);
$color-dark-grey: darken($color-light-grey, 33.33) ;
```

5. We could use an ordinary font such as Sans Serif, but that would look boring – to give our demo a little extra lift, we assign four different font families to variables:

```
// Font families
$pt-sans-family: 'pt_sansregular', sans-serif;
$open-sans-light-family: 'open_sanslight', sans-serif;
$open-sans-regular-family: 'open_sansregular', sans-serif;
$open-sans-bold-family: 'open_sansbold', sans-serif;
```

6. Our demo makes use of a solitary mixin – this takes care of assigning the right font family, size, and color to use, based on the given weight of the font:

```
@mixin fontdetail ($color, $size, $weight) {
  @if $weight == 300 {
```

```
      font-family: $open-sans-light-family;
    } @else if $weight == 400 {
      font-family: $open-sans-regular-family;
    } @else {
      font-family: $open-sans-bold-family;
    }

    color: $color;
    font: {
      size: $size;
      weight: $weight;
    }
  }
```

7. Go ahead and save the file as _variables.scss in the sass
    folder – you can close the file for now, but we will return to it
    during the compilation process.

Although this import file isn't that long, it does start to make use of
Sass functionality – for example, we're using color functions to define
some of the colors used in the palette. It's worth taking a moment to work
through this in greater depth; it will start to come together when we look
at the main style sheet. For now, let's break down the code we've used in
more detail.

Understanding the Imported Code in Detail

In the first partial file we created, we assigned a number of @font-face
declarations – these are used depending on what font weight is assigned
to a particular element. Each declaration uses the standard format for
@font-face; we're merely making use of Sass's ability to import them into
the master style sheet during compilation.

In contrast, the second partial makes use of more Sass functions: we started with defining a number of variables for colors used in the demo. We've used a mix of static and dynamic values; it's important to note that the order is critical, as we make use of static variables to create subsequent colors.

The trick to understanding how the functions work is something we covered back in Chapter 4 – as a reminder, read the function from the inside out. So, for example, the moderate cyan color used is first saturated by 2.4%, before being lightened by 10.39%.

The reason the percentage values are so precise? The values were generated using the Sass color tool at `http://razorltd.github. io/sasscolourfunctioncalculator/` – this tool is worth its weight in gold, when it comes to creating colors!

Moving on, we then assigned four different font families to variables, based on the fonts we set up in the first partial – we make use of PT Sans and Open Sans, the latter of which is in light, bold, and regular type faces. The style sheet is then closed out with a single mixin to assign the right font color, weight, and size, based on the calling declaration in the main style sheet. This uses an `@if...@else` statement to determine that we should use the Light family for a font-weight value of 300, the Regular family for 400, and Bold for a weight value of 700 or higher.

It's at this point we should point out a particular feature in use within this mixin – we have a nested property. This is a simple way to group together multiple styles under a single name (or namespace): each property within that nested block is automatically preceded with the parent name. Take a look at Figure 6-1, where we've grouped two font properties together – our Sassmeister example them compiles them into the font-* properties we know in CSS.

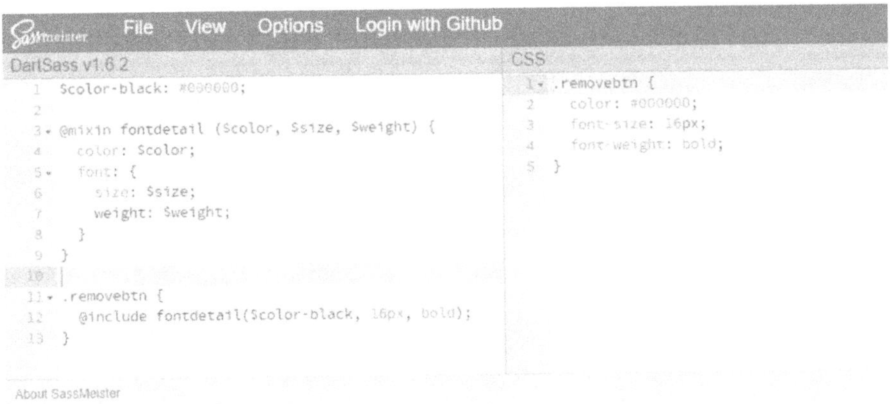

Figure 6-1. *A namespaced nested property*

(In case you're wondering – you can do something similar with lots of properties in Sass, such as border, padding, or margin!)

Okay – it's time, folks: we're at the point where we can create our master style sheet! If you've already read ahead and gasped at the amount of code we're going to cover, then don't worry – it may look a lot, but we'll go through it bit by bit. Much of the code has been nested, with descendant selectors within their respective parent elements – let's dive in and take a look at what we need to set up to make our demo work.

Setting Up the Main Style Sheet

This is where all of the magic happens – there is a fair amount of code, although if you scan through the code, you will hopefully see that much of it has been nested. This makes it easier to read and understand what has been assigned to each parent or descendant element.

Depending on which text editor you use, you may find you can collapse blocks of code – this will also help make it easier to identify the main elements used in the demo.

PUTTING TOGETHER THE MASTER STYLE SHEET

Let's make a start:

1. We'll start by creating a new file – go ahead and save it as `shoppingcart.scss` within the `sass` subfolder of our `shoppingcart` folder.

2. We have a fair amount of code to cover, but we will go through it block by block – start by adding these lines at the top of the file, to call in the import partials we created earlier in this chapter:

```
@import "fonts.scss";
@import "variables.scss";
```

3. Our demo needs some base styles to prepare the ground – leave a line, then add in the four following rules:

```
/* base styles */
body {
  font-family: $pt-sans-family;
  margin: 32px;
  background: $color-light-grey;
  margin: 0;
  padding: 0;
  overflow-x: hidden;
  margin: 32px;
}

.container { margin: 0 auto; width: 980px; }

.clearfix { content: ""; display: table; clear: both; }

h2.exercise { margin-left: auto; margin-right: auto;
width: 980px; }
```

4. With the base rules in place, we can now cover each of the
    principal areas of the cart – we'll start by adding in the rules for
    the cart header:

```scss
/* header */
#site-header {
  margin: 0 auto;
  padding-left: 20px;
  background: $color-white;

  h1 {
    @include fontdetail($color-black, 31px, 300);
    padding: 20px 0;
    position: relative;
    margin: 0;
  }
}
```

5. Next up come the nested rules for the main cart area, including
    product details:

```scss
/* shopping cart */
#cart {
  width: 100%;

  h1 { @include fontdetail($color-black, 25px, 300); }

  p { @include fontdetail($color-black, 18px, 300); }
}

.product {
  border: 1px solid $color-light-grey;
  margin: 20px 0;
  width: 100%;
  position: relative;
  transition: margin .2s linear, opacity .2s linear;
  clear: both;
```

```scss
    & img { width: 100%; height: 100%; }

    .content {
      background-color: $color-white;
      border-bottom: 1px solid $color-description-grey;
      float: left;
      box-sizing: border-box;
      height: 171px;
      padding: 0 20px 0 10px;
      width: 83%;
    }
  }

.product header {
  background-color: $color-white;
  border-bottom: 1px solid $color-description-grey;
  float: left;
  margin: 0 1% 20px 0;
  overflow: hidden;
  padding: 0;
  position: relative;
  width: 153px;
  height: 218px;

  h3 {
    @include fontdetail($color-white, 22px, 300);

    background: $color-moderate-cyan;
    line-height: 49px;
    margin: 0;
    padding: 0 30px;
    position: absolute;
    bottom: -100px;
    right: 0;
    left: 0;
  }
```

```scss
  &:hover img { opacity: .7; }

  &:hover h3 { bottom: 73px; }
}
```

6. Within each product description, we have a details block – this contains the type of book selected, the unit price, quantity selected, and total price for that book. Go ahead and add the following block of code:

```scss
article footer {
  margin: 0;
  padding: 0;
  background-color: $color-almost-white;

  .price {
    @include fontdetail($color-black, 15px, 300);

    background: #fcfcfc;
    float: right;
    line-height: 49px;
    margin: 0;
    padding: 0 30px;

    &:before { content: "$"; }
  }

  .full-price {
    @include fontdetail($color-black, 22px, 400);

    background: $color-yellow;
    float: right;
    line-height: 39px;
    margin: 5px;
    padding: 0 30px;
    transition: margin .15s linear;
```

```scss
        width: 125px;
        text-align: right;

        &:before { content: "$"; }
      }
    }
```

7. The next section takes care of styling the two buttons used to update quantities of items in our basket. Go ahead and add the following lines after the previous section, leaving a blank line first:

```scss
.qt {
  @include fontdetail($color-black, 19px, 300);

  line-height: 50px;
  width: 70px;
  text-align: center;
  display: block;
  float: left;
}

.qt-plus, .qt-minus {
  @include fontdetail($color-black, 30px, 300);

  display: block;
  float: left;
  background: $color-almost-white;
  border: none;
  height: 100%;
  padding: 0 20px;
  transition: background .2s linear;
  line-height: 39px;
  margin: 5px;

  &:hover { background: $color-moderate-cyan;
  color: $color-white; cursor: pointer; }
}
```

8. The next section of our cart is the footer at the bottom of
    the cart – for this, go ahead and leave a line, then add in the
    following styles, to take care of the subtotal, tax, and shipping
    values:

```scss
/* shopping cart footer */
#site-footer {
  background: $color-white;
  margin: 30px 0 0 0;
  padding: 40px 0px;
  width: 100%;
  margin-left: auto;
  margin-right: auto;
  clear: both;

  h1 {
    @include fontdetail($color-black, 25px, 300);

    background: $color-almost-white;
    border-bottom: 1px solid $color-description-grey;
    margin: 0 0 7px 0;
    padding: 14px 40px;
    text-align: center;

    span:before { content: "$"; }
  }

  h2 {
    @include fontdetail($color-black, 24px, 300);

    margin: 10px 0 0 0;
  }

  h3 {
    @include fontdetail($color-black, 19px, 300);
```

```
    margin: 15px 0;
  }
  .left { float: left; }

  .right { float: right; }
}
```

9. We have a few miscellaneous styles, which don't fit in with the nested styles already covered; go ahead and add in the following below the previous style block:

```
button {
  @include fontdetail($color-black, 24px, 400) ;

  background: $color-yellow;
  border: 1px solid $color-dark-grey;
  border-style: none none solid none;
  cursor: pointer;
  display: block;
  padding: 16px 0;
  width: 290px;
  text-align: center;
  transition: all .2s linear;

  &:hover { color: $color-white; background:
  $color-dark-cyan; }
}

.small {
  @include fontdetail($color-black, 13px, 300);

  background: $color-almost-white;
  padding: 10px 16px;
  line-height: 28px;
  border: none;
  display: inline-block;
  line-height: 29px;
}
```

```
.contain { width: 80%; margin-left: auto; margin-right:
auto; }

/* plus and minus buttons in details */
.minus { margin: 0 50px 0 0; }

.added { margin: 0 -50px 0 0; }
```

10. We're almost at the end – this next block styles the remove links and buttons used on the site:

```
/* Remove link over books & remove button in description
*/
a {
color: $color-black;
text-decoration: none;
transition: color .2s linear;

&:hover { color: $color-moderate-cyan; cursor: pointer; }
}
.removebtn {
@include fontdetail($color-black, 16px, bold);

width: 21px;
  float: right;
  margin-top: -72px;
  background-color: $color-light-grey;
  color: $color-white;
  border-radius: 148px;
  text-align: center;
  height: 20px;
  line-height: 20px;

  &:hover {
    cursor: pointer;
    background-color: $color-pure-red;
    transition: background-color 0.3s linear;
  }
}
```

11. The final block takes care of formatting the text displayed in the totals, shipping, and tax values in our cart:

```
/* cart totals */
.carttotal {
  margin: 20px;
  display: inline-block;
  float: right;
  width: 110px;
  margin-top: 13px;

  & > img { width: 40px; height: auto; }

  & > span {
    background-color: $color-very-light-grey;
    padding: 5px 10px;
    border-radius: 20px;
    position: absolute;
    margin-top: 25px;
    margin-left: -20px;
  }
}

.tax, .shipping, .subtotal {
  span {
    float: right;

    &:before { content: "$"; }
  }

  div { width: 100px; display: inline-block; }
}
```

12. Go ahead and save the file – we can close it for the moment, but we will make use of it shortly during the compilation process.

Phew – that was a monster lot of code! Well done if you managed to make it thus far: we've done the hardest and most important part of our demo.

We still have a couple of things to do, though, before we can compile the code and admire our handiwork. First – let's take a breather for a moment, and explore our style sheet code in more detail: it illustrates a few key points you should be aware of when it comes to creating Sass style sheets in your future projects.

Breaking Apart the Code

We could dive straight into our code, but before we do so, I'm going to recommend you do something first: take a breather! Go make yourself a drink, get some fresh air – it does not matter what: the aim though is to get away from the screen for a few minutes.

There is a good reason for doing this: although much of the code we've used in our example is standard CSS, it will at first glance look a little complicated. The key to making it work though is the use of nesting – much of the code within this project was nested to help with readability. With that in mind, let's take a look at the code in detail.

We start with two @import statements – one to import our font declarations, and the second to handle the variables used in our style sheet. We then set up some base styles for our page, including the background for our cart and the title of our exercise.

Next up comes a set of styles for #site-header – this is where we start to use nesting, to include descendant rules for a child h1 element. We then follow this same principle for .product – this includes a host of child rules to style elements within the product description and price sections of the site. Notice though that we also make use of variables for colors – these were defined in the _variables.scss file but are merged in as part of the compilation process.

We then work through a set of declarations for the footer part of each product description; the parent element is article footer, under which we have rules for `.price` and `.full-price` classes. This is swiftly followed by a nested block for the quantity buttons – notice how this also includes a mixin for applying what will be the Open Sans Light font family (as is the case at various points throughout the style sheet).

The next block of nesting in our style sheet is for the `#site-footer` element; this includes declarations for h1, h2, and h3 elements, along with `.left` and `.right` classes to define where the content will sit in the footer. The last part of the style sheet covers a group of miscellaneous styles, before we round out with nested blocks for the cart total values in the footer and tax, shipping, and subtotal values in the footer of our cart.

Tying It All Together

We're almost ready to run the all-important compilation process, but before we do so, there is one more important area to cover: the script code used to make our basket work.

The code we've used is the same as the original version of this cart, save for some minor tweaks and additions – it looks complicated but can be broken down into some clear sections.

The first section (from around lines 5 to 20), is the `changeVal()` function that we use to update prices, depending on how many products have been selected; this is called from various points in our code, as and when we make a change to the quantity of products that have been selected in our cart (or removed). The second function we use is the `changeTotal()` function – this updates the total values (both sub and final), along with shipping and tax costs, before rendering the updated values on screen.

We then have five event handlers set up: the first two take care of responding to clicks on the Remove banner (that appears on books), and the red remove cross in the top right of each product description.

The next two take care of clicks on the plus or minus buttons to add or remove products; these adjust the quantities selected, before calling the changeVal() function to update the total price for the number of copies of the selected book. Our last event handler simply calls the remove function, to either show the placeholder for the checkout process, or indicate if the cart is empty; and therefore, we would not be able to complete the checkout process.

Right – enough chitchat: it's time, folks ... time to see if our demo really works! We've got all of our code in place, so without further ado, let's dive in and run the compilation process.

Compiling Our Code

This is probably one of the easiest parts of this chapter, yet the scariest – does our demo work? Hopefully it will do, but before we find out, it's worth checking through the code to make sure we have everything in place.

If you take a look at the sass subfolder, you should see three files with "finished version" in their names. These are pre-completed versions – you can compare yours with these to see if everything is indeed in place and ready for compilation.

DEMO – COMPILING OUR CODE

Okay – let's make a start on compiling our code. For this, we'll revert back to using the Node.js set up we created at the start of this chapter; let's make a start:

1. Fire up a Node.js terminal session, or revert back to the previous one if you still have it open – make sure the working folder is the shoppingcart folder we set up at the start of this chapter.

2. At the prompt, go ahead and enter `gulp`, then press Enter; you should see it show `Starting 'default'...`, followed by Finished 'default' and a given time.

3. If you try saving the main style sheet now, it will automatically kick in and recompile – an example of this is shown in Figure 6-2.

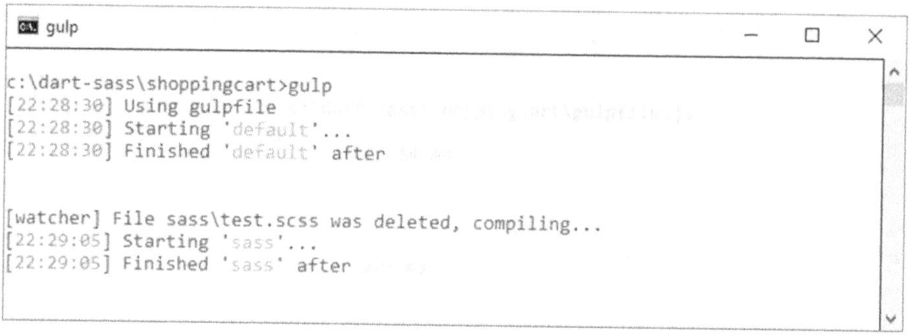

```
c:\dart-sass\shoppingcart>gulp
[22:28:30] Using gulpfile
[22:28:30] Starting 'default'...
[22:28:30] Finished 'default' after

[watcher] File sass\test.scss was deleted, compiling...
[22:29:05] Starting 'sass'...
[22:29:05] Finished 'sass' after
```

Figure 6-2. Compiling our code

Assuming no errors were displayed, then congratulations! You've completed your first project using Sass; sure, there are improvements we can make, but that's fine, as each project should evolve and mature over time. There is just one last thing though...

The Final Result

Hehe – if you were expecting something major, don't worry! That "one last thing" is actually the best part of the whole chapter; this is where we get to see our final result in all its glory. Assuming you encountered no issues, then Figure 6-3 shows the final article, as previewed in a browser.

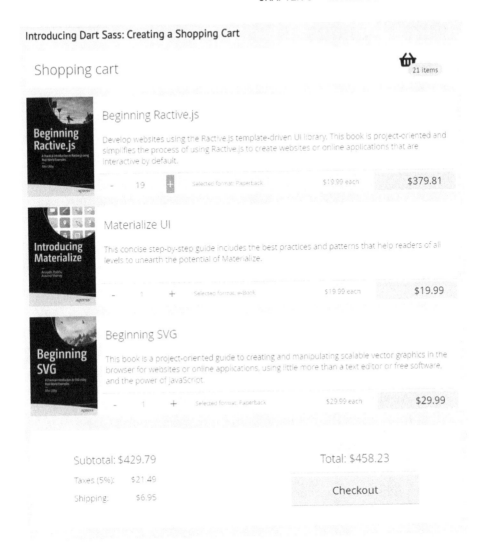

Figure 6-3. *Our finished shopping cart*

It goes to show that we can always make use of Sass within our code –
the exact amount will, of course, depend on the nature of the project, but
that over time we can begin to build up reusable code that can be added to
any number of future projects that make use of Sass.

Future Changes

With our project now operational, the next question we should answer is: Where next ...?

There are a host of changes we could consider – we are only limited by our imagination and the requirements for our project! As Sass is a superset of CSS, it means that we can absolutely convert as much or as little CSS to its Sass equivalent as we like. Once the initial hard work of conversion is done, we can then add in new styles as needed – how about these as a starter for ten?

- We could look at using more namespaced properties – take a look at this extract from the fontdetail mixin:

  ```
  font: {
    size: $size;
    weight: $weight;
  }
  ```

  We already make use of padding and margin throughout the demo, so perhaps there is scope to use this feature?

- A more efficient way of writing colors would be to use a Sass map – we can then group together shades of a color, which will be a more efficient way to write our code. We should take it one step further, though – when we assign color to variable names, use a common format, such as $border-blue-light (generic to specific). It makes it easier to group names, easier for your text editor to suggest color names, and easier to understand where they are being used in your code.

- We could investigate the addition of images such as credit card or security logos – there are several of tools available that we can plug into our Gulpfile.js script, to generate the relevant Sass code for our images.

- We've not really made any use of external libraries in this demo – it doesn't mean to say we shouldn't; how about using the Scut library `https://davidtheclark.github.io/scut/font-face.html`), to handle the @font-face code used in our variables.scss partial file?

- Anyone remember using rem units, instead of pixels? We've used pixel values for convenience throughout, but if you have a hankering for rem units, then Sass can easily add these in using a mixin. Have a look on Google.com for "sass mixin for rem units" – there are dozens of examples!

- We could even go as far as adding in media breakpoints to make our page more responsive – @media queries are handled natively in Sass (and can even be nested); Medium.com has a useful article that explains how you can implement them using Sass, at `https://medium.com/codeartisan/breakpoints-and-media-queries-in-scss-46e8f551e2f2`.

- We've defined a base style .qt for our quantity buttons – this works very well but requires us to assign two styles. How about using the @extend function to create a base style, but then extend it into what we would see as the plus or minus buttons?

These are just some of the ideas that are possible when using Sass – we are, of course, only limited by our imagination! Hopefully this has given you a flavor of what to expect when using Sass in a larger, real-world project; as long as you take care over your planning, use an iterative approach to converting code and are sensible in your choices, then you should have no issue adapting existing projects to using Sass.

Summary

Throughout this book, we've covered a wealth of different features in Sass – from the humble variable right through to building mixins and controlling the output using conditional logic. Over the course of this chapter we've brought many of these features together in the form of a real-world project – our shopping cart may not win any awards, but we must start somewhere! We've covered a fair few tips throughout these pages, so let's take a moment to review what we've learned in this chapter.

We kicked off by outlining details of our project for this chapter, before moving swiftly on to set up our development environment and installing our HTML markup.

Next up, we then explored creating the styles for our project – we worked our way through the two import partials, before assembling the main style sheet. We then brought it all together with a brief look at the jQuery code required to make our cart work, before running the compilation process and viewing the results of our work in a browser.

Phew – what a ride! We've covered a lot throughout this book; I hope you've found it useful, and that you enjoy using Sass just as much as I've enjoyed writing this book!

APPENDIX

Adding Sass to Your Path

The PATH is an important concept when working on the command line. It's a list of directories that tell your operating system where to look for programs, so that you can just write `script` instead of `/home/me/bin/script` or `C:\Users\Me\bin\script`. But different operating systems have different ways to add a new directory to it.

Windows

1. The first step depends which version of Windows that you're using.

2. If you're using Windows 8 or 10, press the Windows key, then search for and select "System (Control Panel)."

3. If you're using Windows 7, right-click the "Computer" icon on the desktop and click "Properties."

4. Click "Advanced system settings."

5. Click "Environment Variables."

© Alex Libby 2019
A. Libby, *Introducing Dart Sass*, https://doi.org/10.1007/978-1-4842-4372-5

6. Under "System Variables," find the PATH variable, select it, and click "Edit." If there is no PATH variable, click "New."

7. Add your directory to the beginning of the variable value followed by a semi-colon. For example, if the value was C:\dart-sass\, add it to the end, as highlighted: it to C:\Users\Me\bin;C:\windows\ system32;**C:\dart-sass**.

8. Click "OK."

9. Restart your terminal.

Mac OS X

1. Open the .bash_profile file in your home directory (for example, /Users/your-user-name/.bash_ profile) in a text editor.

2. Add export PATH="your-dir:$PATH" to the last line of the file, where *your-dir* is the directory you want to add.

3. Save the .bash_profile file.

4. Restart your terminal.

Linux

1. Open the .bashrc file in your home directory (for example, /home/your-user-name/.bashrc) in a text editor.

2. Add export PATH="your-dir:$PATH" to the last line of the file, where *your-dir* is the directory you want to add.

3. Save the .bashrc file.

4. Restart your terminal.

Source: https://katiek2.github.io/path-doc/

Index

9 781484 243718